THE HYMNS OF ABELARD IN ENGLISH VERSE

Translated by

Sister Jane Patricia

UNIVERSITY
PRESS OF
AMERICA

LANHAM • NEW YORK • LONDON

Copyright © 1986 by

University Press of America,® Inc.

4720 Boston Way
Lanham, MD 20706

3 Henrietta Street
London WC2E 8LU England

Library of Congress Cataloging in Publication Data

Abelard, Peter, 1079-1142.
  The hymns of Abelard in English verse.

  Translation of: Hymnarius Paraclithensis.
  Includes bibliographical references.
  1. Hymns, English—Translations from Latin.
2. Hymns, Latin—Translations into English.   I. Jane
Patricia, Sister, 1910-   II. Title.
BV469.A34H9413   1986   264'.2   86-13129
ISBN 0-8191-5480-6 (alk. paper)
ISBN 0-8191-5481-4 (pbk. : alk. paper)

All University Press of America books are produced on acid-free
paper which exceeds the minimum standards set by the National
Historical Publications and Records Commission.

To

ST. GREGORY'S ABBEY

Three Rivers, Michigan

PREFACE

The complexity of Abelard's thought was apparently as disturbing to Abelard himself as it was to contemporary ecclesiastics. The unfinished state of his theologies is in contrast to his older contemporary, Anselm of Canterbury, who at Bec and at Canterbury produced organized and complete works with satisfaction to himself and his students. The pleasure he took in the finality of his work contrasts with the restless searching of Abelard's mind, whose efforts to elucidate his theology have been followed by students through the eight centuries since he taught and wrote, but his hymns have lain in the original Latin. Their study shows them as convoluted and as condensed as anything he wrote, packed with allusion and doctrine. To keep his own meter means to keep the condensation and to present his didactic temper as Eloise and her nuns appreciated it.

In this effort to present the hymns anglice, I acknowledge the resources of the libraries of Rutgers and Princeton Universities as well as the seminaries in New Brunswick and Princeton; the Centre D'Etudes Supérieures de Civilisation Médiévale at Poitiers and the Graduate Centre for Medieval Studies at Reading University in England; the British Library in London and those of Smith College and Amherst College in the States. I am particularly grateful to the Reverend J. H. W. Rhys of St. Luke's School of Theology in Sewanee, Tennessee, as the first to encourage me in the attempt at translation, and to Professor Stephen Brown, now at Boston College, who read the whole text critically; to the Mother House of my convent in Windsor in England for their patience with my unscheduled way of life; and finally to St. Gregory's Abbey in Michigan for their understanding of an interest in study as essential to the religious life.

TABLE OF CONTENTS

THE HYMNS IN ENGLISH VERSE .

INTRODUCTION

The appearance of Peter Abelard at the end of the eleventh century heralded an intellectual movement of keen excitement and inquiry that was to give to his lifetime the name of the Twelfth Century Renaissance.[1]

Western Europe was entering a stage of quickened development and expanding horizons, in which the church was grappling with the astonishing ideas of Aristotle that emerged in small portions through the translations of the Moslem world to mingle with and be reconciled to the early church Fathers as well as scripture.[2]

Abelard was born in 1079, the eldest son of a knight living in Le Pallet near Nantes in Brittany, possessing lands under the feudal rights of support and protection from his lord and toward his own dependents. The father was a man of letters, tied to his properties, but not at all averse to his son's pursuit of a scholarly life, so that Peter was sent to Loches to study under the then famous Roscelin, known later for his invention of nominalism, the controversial philosophy that gave him the reputation of tritheism.[3]

The belief in the existence of absolute values came from Plato's statements on ideas and troubled the thinkers of the day, giving it religious importance in the definition of the Trinity. Roscelin claimed that absolutes are only names, noises, a breath; whereas Anselm of Canterbury maintained that universals are the reality, and individual objects are only shadows. Anselm in his De fide Trinitatis[4] attacked the nominalist position saying that if individuals constitute reality, the Trinity could not be said to

----

1. Charles Homer Haskins, The Renaissance of the Twelfth Century (Harvard 1927).

2. G. Paré, A. Brunet, and P. Tremblay, La Renaissance du douzième siècle (Paris 1933), pp. 138-145.

3. N.M. Gorce, A. Vacant, Dictionnaire de théologie catholique (DTC) 13, 2911.

4. Anselm, De fide Trinitatis, Patrologia Latina (PL) 158, 250-284.

exist. Abelard parted company from Roscelin and from the realist side as well, standing in a middle position on concepts as real, though his name was linked with Roscelin's, to his own damage later.[5]

He then went to Paris in 1100 to study under William of Champeaux, the archdeacon, but the young student soon outdistanced his teacher who retired to the Abbey of St. Victor on the left bank for contemplation and writing. Abelard lectured at Corbeil and Melun, near Paris, making himself the center of what eventually became the university. By his own admission students flocked to him and spread his renown into wider areas.[6]

The University at that time was indeed "without walls," consisting only of teachers who could successfully attract student listeners. There were no buildings other than what the lecturer had at his disposal, no living quarters, no libraries as we know them. Abelard's audiences grew from the students' interest in the philosophy he taught and in the charm of his own convictions and persuasiveness. The "nations" that later separated into ethnic and often antagonistic groups were students from England, Germany, Italy and farther who heard of Abelard's reputation and sat under his lectures and participated in discussions. John of Salisbury, the Englishman respected for his learning and judgment, was his pupil at Mont Ste. Geneviève and reported that Abelard was a "clarus doctor," and that he, John, had taken in all he could with the whole grasp of his mind.[7]

A student from Brescia in Italy was one Arnold, a tireless reformer who won Abelard's sympathy by his demand for freedom of judgment, but Arnold's direction was toward the government of the communes while Abelard

----

5. Meyrick Carré, Realists and Nominalists (Oxford 1964), p. 40. See also G.R. Evans, Anselm and Talking about God (Oxford 1978), p. 40.

6. Historia calamitatum (HC) PL 178, 116-118.

7. PL 199, 867B.

wanted to use reason in theology.[8] Arnold's criticisms
of the church brought him to the point of saying that
it was no longer the body of Christ; but it was his
political speeches that brought condemnation and later
burning, while Abelard's insistence on the use of human
reason condemned him also, though not to death.

When Abelard was about thirty-five his fame was
such that Canon Fulbert of Notre Dame in Paris asked
him to teach his niece and ward Eloise.   Her
intelligence was a match even for his, and a challenge
which he gladly undertook. He was soon in love with
her, and played on the canon's guilelessness to arrange
to live in the same house.[9] He was writing love songs
for her, sung in the streets of Paris, as she reminds
him in a letter, songs of which we may have some
fragments, though it is impossible to be sure that they
are Abelard's.   It was the period of the troubadors
when the clergy as well as students were writing erotic
verse, and the Goliards, so called from their god
Golias, representing gluttony, were popular in love
songs.[10]

It was not long before Eloise was pregnant. The
canon was enraged at the duplicity of his niece and of
the instructor he had provided, to such an extent that
Abelard sent Eloise to his own sister in Brittany until
the son was born whom they called by the strange name
of Astrolabe, an indication of the new knowledge in
science. Eloise was still in her teens and subject to
the canon, so that at the uncle's insistence they were
married secretly.[11] Eloise objected that the marriage

----

8. G.W. Greenaway, Arnold of Brescia (Cambridge 1931),
   pp. 141-144; 150; 157-158; 165-167.

9. HC, PL 178, 122.

10. F.J.E. Raby, Christian Latin Poetry (Oxford 1927),
    pp. 273-277.

11. Nothing more is known of Astrolabe except the open
    letter in elegiacs his father wrote him as he was
    growing up, in reality a general letter on
    education. PL 178, 1750-1766.

would hinder Abelard's career,[12] but to please the uncle she consented. Fulbert could not then keep it secret, breaking his promise, whereupon Abelard became concerned at the unhappiness of Eloise under her uncle's roof and persuaded her to return to the nuns of Argenteuil where she had been in school. Fulbert took the move to mean Abelard's rejection of her and bribed a servant to let in hired men at night to castrate Abelard in order to prevent his receiving higher orders.[13] As a Master in the schools, he was already a cleric, on his way to ordination as a priest and probably higher preferment, but the church was enforcing its rule against married clergy.[14]

After the sad disgrace Abelard entered the abbey of St. Denis to become a Benedictine monk, but he soon antagonized the monks by giving them Bede's opinion that Dionysius, their patron St. Denis, had been bishop of Corinth and not of Athens. What seems a matter of slight importance was taken as a denigration of their house, so that he fled the abbey for a time,[15] but returned with an apology for what seemed a mistake of Bede's.

His writing On the Unity and Trinity of God received wider attention about 1120, and, coupled with his dialectical method of teaching, aroused the suspicion of ecclesiastical authorities, who called him to Soissons in 1121. Some of the alarming statements were that Abelard taught that the Holy Spirit is not of the same substance as the Father; that Christ did not take flesh that he might free us from the devil's yoke; and that the cause of the incarnation was to illuminate the world and inflame it with his love. A disturbing opinion was that those who crucified Christ in

----

12. Ep. 2, PL 178, 184D-185A. "Excellentiae tuae gloriam minus laederem."

13. HC PL 178, 129-134.

14. T.P. McLaughlin, "The Prohibition of Marriage Against Canons in the Early Twelfth Century," in Medieval Studies (Toronto 1941), vol. 3, pp. 94-100; see p. 94.

15. HC PL 178, 155A. "Illi vehementer accensi clamare ceperunt." 1550C "Nocte latenter aufugi."

4

ignorance did not sin; and he was quoted as saying that omnipotence belongs especially to the Father. Some of the accusations were from students who may have misunderstood him, and some were from Abelard's writings taken out of context.[16]

At Soissons in 1121 there were no theologians of Abelard's ability; he had "a sharper mind and a different temperament . . . He belonged to a younger generation of more thoroughgoing dialecticians,"[17] and therefore he could not argue his case with any hope of understanding. The ecclesiastics were headed by a papal legate with the full power of Pope Calixtus II, and the result was a condemnation of Abelard's book on the Trinity, and the requirement that he burn it with his own hand.[18] The unfairness of being condemned without a hearing fell heavily on a man of his sensitivity and keen intelligence. He describes his anger and the tears on his face as he burned it, and the sobs that almost prevented him from reciting the Athanasian creed as they demanded.[19] The punishment was that he be immured in the monastery of St. Médard near Paris, but the abbot of St. Denis allowed his return to his former place after a short time.[20] He was permitted to withdraw for a while to a retreat on the Seine later called the Paraclete.

His next move was to the abbey of St. Gildas in Brittany, his home country, where one would think he might feel some relaxation, but he found the monastery difficult to rule and impossible to reform, even though the monks elected him abbot. They regretted their

----

16. PL 178, 1049-1054.

17. Beryl Smalley, The Study of the Bible in the Middle Ages (Oxford 1952), p. 51.

18. The book was the De Unitate et Trinitate divina from which came the Theologia christiana c. 1123, and then the Introductio ad theologiam c. 1125. C.J. Hefele and H. Leclercq, eds., Histoire des conciles (Paris 1913), vol. 5, pp. 593-602.

19. HC PL 178, 149C. H-L reports only Abelard's own words for this council.

20. HC PL 178, 154-155.

choice and even tried to kill him.[21] His hymn # 119 relates the life of St. Gildas, a pioneer in the uncultivated territory of Brittany, as difficult a task as was Abelard's in his century. Abelard calls him a lamp placed on a stand and a star for sailors, who guided the uncultured inhabitants by his kindness and his fides intrepida. The land was barbarous, and the language unknown to Abelard, the life of the monks was shameful and unruly, and the people of the country inhuman and disorganized.

The abbey of St. Denis had lost its abbot by death and was now ruled by the famous Abbot Suger, counsellor of kings, builder and artist, responsible for the present abbey church of St. Denis and the inspiration of Chartres Cathedral. Suger read the deeds of his abbey and discovered that the lands of Argenteuil, where Eloise was, belonged of right to the abbey of St. Denis, which meant that the Argenteuil nuns must be evacuated. When Abelard heard of it, he brought Eloise and her nuns to his small place near Nogent-sur-Seine where his students had built a few poor shelters. He was able to provide better quarters for them, so that the Abbey was confirmed and dedicated to the Paraclete in 1131 and blessed by Pope Innocent II.[22] Bernard, Cistercian abbot of Clairvaux, though fearful of anything from Abelard's hand as heretical, visited the abbey under Eloise and could find no fault greater than that they used the word supersubstantialem in the Lord's Prayer instead of cotidianum.[23]

In 1132 Abelard left St. Gildas to save his life, and it was then that he wrote the Historia calamitatum, long after the events it narrates. It does not seem reasonable that Eloise should ascribe her actions, as she does in a letter reported by Abelard in this Historia, entirely to love of Abelard instead of God,

----

21. HC PL 178, 165-166, 180B.

22. HC PL 178, 168-170.

23. Ep. 10 of Abelard to Bernard, PL 178, 335-340. Abelard explains that he follows Matthew rather than Luke because the former gives seven petitions and Luke five, and he adds that supersubstantialem is a better translation of the Greek 'επιούσιον. PL 178, 337.

when her further life showed devotion to her abbey and to her nuns even in Abelard's lifetime.[24] J. Benton and others have suggested that Abelard may have altered the letters or depended on a faulty memory. He was undeniably vain, speaking of his fame with his students and denigrating other teachers. Muckle says, "Most of his troubles were caused by his pride."[25]

During the establishment of the abbey of the Paraclete, Eloise wrote to Abelard for guidance in adapting the rule of St. Benedict to women, ending with an appealing, "Do tell us, and we'll listen."[26] In his response Abelard makes commonsense adjustments as to clothes and food, field work, chaplaincies by monks, and departmental responsibilities. In another letter he discusses reading and study, giving the nuns a review of classical literature as well as of the Fathers and the Bible for their mental training and devotion.[27] It is not very different from Jerome's letters to Eustochium and Laeta.[28] Abelard's own experience in St. Gildas and St. Denis showed him what a breakdown in discipline can do, and therefore he includes preventive regulations in his rule for the Paraclete:

> Foreseeing as much as we can of this plague, we forbid absolutely that any superior shall live more delicately or with more ease than the nuns . . . but should do all things with the flock committed to her.[29]

----

24. Ep. 2, PL 178, 186. See also R.W. Southern, "The Letters of Abelard and Eloise," in Medieval Humanism and Other Studies (N.Y. 1970), pp. 86-104.

25. J.T. Muckle, The Story of Abelard's Adversities (Toronto 1954), p. 7.

26. PL 178, 226; Letter 6. "Loquere tu nobis, et audiemus."

27. Letter 9. PL 178, 325-336.

28. PL 178, 273BC.

29. PL 178, 273BC.

The Benedictine rule requires some four hours of reading a day, but with few books available, it came to mean being read to, and with manuscript books the reading was difficult and slow. The meaning of the words was savored in meditation.[30]

As far as one can tell, the nuns at the Paraclete welcomed his solicitude for their spiritual and material well-being, taking their part in the eleventh-century revival which David Knowles said "is perhaps the most widespread and the most spiritual of all the mysterious religious revivals of the West."[31] When we think of the things a woman of Abelard's time had lived through, we can understand his interest in the women who were martyrs and confessors. Two crusades took many of the men away for years at a time, and some never returned; there had been recurring famines because of weather and climate; the plague that later wiped out a large part of Europe had sent its messengers many times in Abelard's century with less destruction but fearsome suffering; wars small and great involved the knightly class.

Recognition of women's value began in the eleventh century with devotion to the Blessed Virgin Mary and the dedication of many churches to her. While church patrons had previously been chosen from many walks of life, St. Mary Magdalen for Vézelay, St. Sernin the bishop for Toulouse, St. Stephen for the Conqueror's abbey in Caen, the Trinity for Mathilda's, St. Lazare at Autun, St. Peter in Poitiers; with the building of the Gothic cathedral in Chartres in the twelfth century all eyes were turned to the Blessed Virgin, and church after church claimed her as patron, Paris, Amiens, Beauvais, Bourges, and others. Her devotion grew into the next century to become a characteristic Franciscanism, the "emotional identification with the divine mother at the foot of the cross that gave impetus to the devotional tide which swept through

----

30. Ruth Cosby, "Oral Delivery in the Middle Ages," in Speculum III 1936, pp. 88-110.

31. David Knowles, From Pachomius to Ignatius (Oxford 1966), p. 16.

Europe for two centuries."[32] Abelard's Christmas hymns, # 30-33, concern St. Mary as well as the four additional hymns for her feasts, proclaiming "the adoration which gathered around the persons of the Virgin in heaven and the lady on earth."[33] In his first sermon Abelard writes "[The Lord] determined to assume the form of our sex from a woman, that in both sexes there might be grace, as in both came guilt."[34] To select Eloise as a representative woman would be a mistake, for Christopher Brooke believes her to be "so exceptional a person as to be the worst possible basis for any generalization,"[35] and Henry Osborn Taylor speaks of her strong mind with its grasp and its capacity for reasoning. She was "a great woman, possessed of an admirable mind, a character which proved its strength through years."[36] The convent's neighbors liked Eloise and helped her and sought instruction from her. Letters of others express admiration for her, and Peter the Venerable wrote, "From the most humble lay people to the courtiers of the Pope, all considered her as a mother . . . they sought her presence and interviews, noting her prudence and the incomparable sweetness of her patience."

Papal bulls are extant giving privileges and exemptions to the Paraclete and the abbess, and King Louis VI gave privileges in 1135. The bishop of Melun spoke of the devout service of the nuns, and the archbishop of Sens wrote of "Eloise, venerable abbess and all the very holy convent." From its foundation it received much land and gifts from Count Thibaut of Champagne and others. The abbess was known to be conciliatory, and she established peace in a certain

----

32. J.A.W. Bennett, Poetry of the Passion (Oxford 1982) pp. 34-35.

33. Eileen Power, Medieval Women ed. M.M. Postan, (Cambridge 1975) p. 10.

34. PL 178, 380.

35. Christopher Brooke, Medieval Church and Society (N.Y.U. 1972) p. 97.

36. Henry Osborn Taylor, The Medieval Mind, (Harvard 1962), vol. II, pp. 29, 46.

litigation in 1144. At her death there were six dependent houses.[37]

Abelard was established on Mont Ste. Geneviève in 1135 with John of Salisbury as his pupil, away from the Ile de la Cité, when probably he wrote the Dialogue Between a Philosopher, a Jew and a Christian, reflecting the toleration of the Jews in northern France noted by Beryl Smalley.[38] He was again charged with heresy and summoned to a council at Sens, the diocesan center, in 1140. Bernard of Clairvaux became anxious for the cause of orthodoxy when he read a letter from a Benedictine abbot, William of St. Thierry, reporting what seemed heresy in the teaching of Abelard. Written in 1139,[39] it presented the first knowledge of Abelard's intransigence, and urges Geoffrey of Chartres and Bernard to action; Bernard in his acknowledgement asks time to consider it. William lists thirteen points of questionable doctrine, complaining throughout of "unheard of novelties," "novel senses which he puts upon received terms," and "recurring novelties." Nova docet, nova scribit. Bernard in 1140 summoned the bishops of the diocese to Sens, for as Otto of Freising said, "Bernard detested those teachers who might put too much reliance on human reason and worldly wisdom," and Otto himself felt that Abelard was "so arrogant, and had such confidence in his own abilities, that he would scarcely descend from his intellectual height to listen to teachers."[40]

In 1140 Bernard wrote to Pope Innocent II protesting against the works of Abelard, urging the Pope to read them at first hand, those about the Trinity, the Scito te ipsum or Ethics,[41] and the "Sentences," which is probably the Sic et non, a compilation of contradictory opinions from the Bible

----

37. Charlotte Charrier, Héloise dans l'histoire et dans la légende (Paris 1933), pp. 7, 178, 256-275, 289.

38. Smalley, p. 150.

39. PL 182, 531-533; see 531.

40. J. Mabillon, ed. Life and Works of St. Bernard, tr. J. Eales (London 1939), p. 539.

41. PL 182, 351-254.

and from the Fathers, in which he offered no solution but presented them as a challenge to contemporary intellects. Some scholars have argued that Gratian, the organizer of canon law, took his position in the development of scholastic theology from Abelard.[42] In the next letter to the Pope Bernard is anxious for the effects these writings will have on the church, for "his books fly abroad," and they have passed "from nation to nation . . . a new Gospel is being fashioned . . . a new faith . . . and everything is given in a perverse spirit, in an unprecedented manner, and beyond what we have received." The puzzlement and the shock of novelties is evident.[43]

After the condemnation at the council, Bernard asked the pope for confirmation and sentencing.[44] He urges Anselm's ontological argument as a basis for authority, which should be sufficient without Abelard's dialectical devices, and he complains that Abelard "defines faith as private judgment."[45] He includes fourteen heads of heresies, some of which Abelard denied entirely, others of which he explained in their context. Bernard wrote to Ivo of Chartres, "Master Peter Abelard, a monk without a rule, a prelate without a cure, . . . within a Herod, without a John . . . having nothing of the monk but the name and habit."[46]

When Abelard realized the circumstances, he cut off his planned defense and appealed to Rome. Bernard and the clergy knew he was an able speaker who could defend his theology by argument, and this they wished to prevent by their condemnation in advance; but the appeal came as a surprise to them and took it out of

----

42. Stanley Chodorow, Christian Political Theory and Church Politics in the Mid-12th Century (University of California 1972).

43. Mabillon, p. 545. PL 182, 1053-1072.

44. Mabillon, Letter 190, pp. 565-591.

45. Mabillon, pp. 569, 574, 583.

46. Mabillon, Letter 193, p. 594.

their hands.[47]   Innocent II agreed to their judgment
and condemned Abelard's teaching.[48]

Abelard began his journey to Rome to plead his
case, but he came on the way to the abbey of Cluny,
then under Peter the Venerable. Peter's letter to Pope
Innocent II after Abelard's death tells how he
persuaded Abelard to remain at Cluny instead of
pursuing his purpose.[49] Whether there was distrust of
the pope on the abbot's part or not, it was a gesture
of charity, for the nearly two years that Abelard spent
there were a time of peaceful study and teaching.

When Peter the Venerable called on the abbot of
Citeaux to arrange a meeting between Abelard and
Bernard, it softened the old antagonism into a
reconciliation. As Abelard showed signs of illness,
the Abbot Peter sent him to a Cluniac house at Marcel-
lès-Chalons for better air, and there he died in April
of 1142.   Eloise survived him by twenty years, as
abbess of the Paraclete, respected by her own nuns and
consulted by bishops and clergy.

Peter the Venerable wrote to Eloise of Abelard's
last days, describing him as always held in honor, a
true servant and philosopher of Christ and a teacher;
none was like him in humility; it was amazing that a
man of such repute could so abase himself. With him
study was continuous, prayer frequent, silence
constant; steadfastly mild and humble, he thus passed
over to the Lord.[50]

D.E. Luscombe has summed up the story in a
paragraph:

Most reputable masters and most monks lived
settled lives; Abelard's was turbulent in the
extreme. He appeared to scoff and to insult.

----

47. Hefele and Leclercq, vol. 5, pp. 593-602.

48. Geoffrey Barraclough, The Medieval Papacy (New York
    1968) page 100.

49. PL 189, 305-306, Ep. 4.

50. Giles Constable, The Letters of Peter the Venerable
    (Harvard 1967) vol. 1, no. 115, pp. 306-307.

He was twice condemned for heresy . . . He
fathered a child, and although he was a
master, he married and then dismissed his
wife. He was castrated as the result of a
personal enmity. He was punished by being
ordered to enter a monastery, from which he
fled. He was an abbot until attempts were
made upon his life. Yet he became in his
last days an exemplary and pious Cluniac.[51]

There are many lives of Abelard, of which the most
authoritative is still that of Charles Remusat, Abélard
(Paris 1945) in two volumes. There are also:

Gandillac, M., Oeuvres choisis d'Abélard (Paris 1945)
Gilson, Etienne, La philosophie au moyen age (Paris
1944)
Grane, Leif, Peter Abélard (New York 1970)
Luscombe, D.E., The School of Peter Abelard (Cambridge
1969)
Monfrin, J., Abelard's 'Historia Calamitatum' (Paris
1967)
Murray, A.V., Abelard and St. Bernard (Manchester
University, 1967)
Sikes, J.G., Peter Abailard (Cambridge 1932)

----

51. D.E. Luscombe, Peter Abelard's 'Ethics' (Oxford
    1971), p. xii.

THEOLOGY

Abelard was a Benedictine monk, of the royal abbey of St. Denis, and then for some ten years abbot of the monastery of St. Gildas in Brittany, finally dying under the gentle rule of Peter the Venerable at the great abbey of Cluny. Benedictine life was his choice, and his means of spirituality, a life centered on worship with opportunity for corporate and private devotion.

Augustine, bishop of Hippo in the fifth century, whose rule influenced Benedict in forming his in the sixth, gathered his clergy around him for the work of the cathedral, having a common table and a common purse, though each man had his own parish work of teaching and preaching and visiting, dedicated to the vita apostolica although the term does not appear until later.[1] Celtic theology, individual and sometimes erratic, came through Wales to Iona and Lindisfarne and down into Brittany in the Celtic peregrinatio pro Christo.[2] Charlemagne's son, Louis the Pious, had regularized the Benedictine life with Benedict of Aniane in the ninth century, who gave his estates for a royal abbey near the capitol of Aachen, and in the following century the abbey of Cluny was founded in 910 in which all the Benedictine life of Europe was to coalesce, under a remarkable succession of capable abbots with ties to the ruling house of France and to the papacy.

Cluny lost the allegiance of a group of monks who in 1098, complaining of the elaboration of church Offices and the lack of manual labor, left to establish a house at Citeaux from whose name they took their title of Cistercians. Claiming still the Benedictine rule, they welcomed the devout without regard to education, so that the conversi, as they came to be called from their adult response, came in enormous enthusiasm and gave impetus to the clearing and draining of land for productive farming. Their Carta

----

1. Jean Leclercq, Etudes sur le vocabulaire monastique du moyen age. Studia Anselmiana #46 (Rome 1961), p. 38.

2. Timothy Fry, ed., The Rule of St. Benedict: RB 1980 (Collegeville, Minn. 1981), ch. 67.

caritatis emphasized the relationship of love as against the indulgence with which they charged the older monasteries.

The Benedictine Rule gives first place to the Opus Dei, the Offices of worship,[3] through which the monk gives voice to his belief in and dependence on God in the Trinity. Abelard came to grief over his doctrine of the Trinity, condemned at the synod of Soissons in 1121 and at the council of Sens in 1140 as heretical for his subjective judgments, though he has been acquitted of that charge and was exonerated by Pope Innocent II after his death at the request of Abbot Peter the Venerable.[4] One of the first of Abelard's writings was the Introductio in theologiam which begins with the emphasis on Unity in Trinity.[5] Almost every one of these hymns has its doxology, its praise of the Trinity. The very word theologia was of doubtful connotation since it had pagan associations and meant a mystical knowledge of God, experienced by only a few. "Theologia in its proper sense, as the Fathers used it, is not so much knowledge about God, but knowledge of God through communion with Him and contemplation of Him,"[6] and "is the realm of prayer," a movement of progress.[7] This was not new, for it had appeared in Bede where theology is equated with contemplation,[8] but it took the next century to use the word in the sense in which we know it.

Abelard's attribution of power to the Father, wisdom to the Son, and goodness to the Spirit was too much like a separation of the three persons, though he

----

3. Adalbert de Vogüé, La règle de Saint Benoît (Paris 1972) tr. Jean Neufville; vol.1, pp. 412-491; vol. II, pp. 508-674.

4. DTC, 13, 2911.

5. PL 178, 987.

6. Andrew Louth, The Origins of the Christian Mystical Experience (Oxford 1981) p. 164.

7. Leclercq, Etudes, pp. 70-79.

8. PL 92, 455.

called them relationships and not differences.[9] His naming of the retreat, later Eloise's convent, for the Paraclete was disliked because its selection of one person of the Trinity seemed disrespectful.

The depth of Abelard's thought is perhaps best shown in his writing on what we now call the theory of the Atonement, though to him it was no theory or organized proposition but a description of the "work of Christ."[10] Bernard of Clairvaux, the great apostle of love, preached in his sermon # 20 that God first loved us, and his love is the incentive to ours; but he went on to describe the snare of deceptions that Christ deliberately laid down for the devil in order to catch him,[11] a proposition that Abelard dismissed out of hand, even taking exception to Augustine's standpoint that the crucifixion cancelled the debt.[12] Anselm of Canterbury, almost the only thinker whom Abelard admired, taught in his Cur Deus homo that the sacrifice was necessary for man's redemption.[13] Abelard noted for refutation also the Moralia of Gregory the Great who treated redemption principally as a liberation to humanity from bondage to the devil, as though the devil had rights of his own.[14] In the Easter hymn (# 58, 3) Abelard may be referring to this when he says, "Fraus in hamo fallitur," the scheme of the trap fails, but he never suggests a ransom or price paid to anyone, to Satan or to God.[15]

----

9. Grane, pp. 96, 98. Cf. Job 12, 13: "Apud ipsum est sapientia et fortitudo; ipse habet consilium et intelligentiam." (Vulgate).

10. Murray, p. 117.

11. PL 183, 867-972

12. J.R. McCallum, Abelard's Christian Theology (Oxford 1948) p. 103.

13. PL 158, 361-364; 903.

14. PL 76, 680.

15. Richard Weingart, The Logic of Divine Love (Oxford 1970), p. 138. In sermon V Abelard says, "This love, when it makes us willingly do what the Son

Abelard's new departure is his exemplarist view of
the atonement, that Christ's example as a man shows us
the love of God and draws us to love in return, which
love on our part stirs us to put aside sin and to
desire the full love of God. "The revelation of the
cross was that of divine love inciting to responsive
love in conduct of life."[16] We love God because we
love beatitude, and he is beatitude.[17] All the Good
Friday hymns, # 42-51, express gratitude for the love
of God beyond measure. The reader can find no mention
whatever of the conflict between the goodness and
justice of God.

Related to this doctrine of Abelard's is his
conviction that sin is internal, and is the refusal,
the despising, of God, a personal and an individual
offense.[18] He quotes from Romans 3.22, "It is the same
justice of God that comes through faith to everyone,
Jew and pagan alike, who believes in Jesus Christ," to
point up the responsibility of each one for himself.
It is the love of Mary Magdalen for the Lord that
brings thorough repentance, expressed in hymn # 128.
The remission of sin is in repentance, not in acts.[19]

Forty-nine of Abelard's hymns on saints, singly
and collectively, survive, and although there are
probably more of his hymns that have been lost to us,
these suffice to explain his doctrine. In all these
hymns about martyrs and confessors, male and female, he
is intent on assuring us that the merit comes from God
only, not from human effort but through grace alone.
The doxology of # 85 for the feast of apostles ascribes

----

has taught, adopts us among the sons." PL 178, 423
D.

16. McCallum, p. 103.

17. Etienne Gilson, Théologie mystique de S. Bernard
    (Paris 1934), p. 184

18. Jean Baptiste Kors, La justice primitive et le
    péché originel d'après St. Thomas (Kain, Belgium
    1922) p. 36.

19. C.W. Bynum, "Did the Twelfth Century Discover the
    Individual?" in Journal of Ecclesiastical History
    (Cambridge 1980) Jan. 1980, vol. 31, 1.

glory to God alone, and # 87 begins with the statement of subordination of kings to the Lord. St. Paul in # 91 is "drawing thunder from heaven steadily," and St. John the Evangelist is the eagle "sheltered safe in the Lord's divinity." The doxology of the feast of martyrs says, (# 97, 3) "Father, whose gifts they are, yours is the holiness," and # 110 for confessors, "All good deeds of these are gifts only in your grace."

The Eucharist is a rare subject in Abelard's poetry, perhaps as Dr. Szöverffy suggests, because of the current heresy of Berengar of Tours, who some fifty years before Abelard's birth attacked in writing and in sermons the standard doctrine of transubstantiation in much the same way as did the protestants of the sixteenth century.[20] The Benedictines throughout the controversy were the defenders of the catholic interpretation, led by Pope Gregory VII who insisted on the tradition from Augustine, "Crede ut intellegas," believe so that you may understand.[21] Edward Schillebeeckx of our time has described the thought when "The ordinary people of the Middle Ages had no idea at all of what was happening in the universities." "Most people in the church continued to think about the Eucharist in the way that had already been in existence for centuries and had been brought about largely by the great Pope Gregory I . . . who had, to a great extent, been responsible for giving it its moving naivety."[22]

The hymns Abelard wrote to be used in Eloise's convent for the performance of the divine Office, which is in itself an extension of the Eucharist, are all mindful of the theology of the day or of the season.

No real liturgy is possible without an authentic experience of Christ in his mystery . . . The whole thrust of the church's liturgical reform is in the direction of

----

20. HP vol. 1, p. 126. Raoul Heurtevant, Durand de Troarn et les origines de l'hérésie bérengarienne (Paris 1911) p. 116 f.

21. Augustine, sermon 43, PL 38, 258.

22. Edward Schillebeeckx, The Eucharist (London 1968) tr. D.T. Smith, pp. 11-58. See also Flèche-Martin, Histoire de l'église' vol. 13, 40; A. Forest.

making it possible for the mystery of Christ to find a living, fruitful expression in and through the church. [23]

Abelard's hymns use symbolism in his effort to express the mystery of Christ, and are a clear sign of the intellectual ferment of his century, reaching out to symbols as ways to the truth.[24] He admired the eloquence of the Bible in Jerome's translation from the veritas hebraica for Latin readers, and used it to show that scripture was compatible with philosophy,[25] as Origen in the third century had used symbolism to harmonize the Old and New Testaments. The very words Amen and Alleluia are symbols, without in the latter word a translatable meaning. St. Paul in his letter to the Galatians[26] used the Old Testament story of Hagar and Sarah as the two covenants.[27] The contemporary translations of the East from the Greek and the Hebrew which were appearing in Toledo brought exciting and unheard-of meanings from biblical studies.

The four senses of interpretation are traditionally historical, allegorical, tropological, and anagogical, though generally writers see scripture in two ways, the literal and the allegorical, which latter includes the tropological or moral sense, and the anagogical or eschatological. The literal reading gives the facts; the allegorical shows us what to believe; the moral how to live; and the anagogical points the contemplative way. Origen had written, "A homily of divine scripture is like a seed . . . it

----

23. Chrysogonus Waddell, "Origin and Early Evolution of the Cistercian Antiphonary," in M. Basil Pennington, ed., The Cistercian Spirit (Shannon 1970), pp. 190-223; see p. 223.

24. Henri de Lubac, Exégèse Médiévale (Paris 1959), vol. 1, p. 269.

25. Smalley, p. 8.

26. Gal 4.24-26, 31.

27. Gen 21.8-21.

grows into a stalk, it multiplies . . . it grows into a tree."[28]

In his second preface, before hymn # 30, Abelard calls attention to the fact that the hymns of the night Offices (Matins) deal with the work of creation, but those of the day Hours (Lauds and the Little Hours) bring their allegorical and moral explanation.[29] "Abelard's novelty is the introduction of a third constituent element in the diurnal hymns, parallels drawn with the stages of human development from childhood onward."[30] The Venerable Bede had developed this triple symbolism, as Abelard doubtless knew, since he was a reader of Bede,[31] but he carries it through all these hymns of creation.

Hymns # 3 through 9 give the sequence of the events of creation; in those up to # 30 Abelard uses the symbol of light frequently. # 11, 1 speaks of the morning star, of dawn, of the sun, with its interpretation. He follows a long line of mystical writers in transferring the city of Jerusalem to the realization of the city of God in heaven, the home and goal of our life. The elaborate description in the Apocalypse has antecedents in Ezekiel, and in Isaiah who speaks of the city of Zion, no longer of a garden as in Genesis.[32] Abelard boasts in the Historia calamitatum of his understanding of Ezekiel.[33] Augustine's two cities were well known to him, and his best known hymn, "O quanta, qualia," # 29, is about the sabbath in Jerusalem. In # 38 Sion is the church and the bride of Christ. In his sermon # V he equates the rib of Adam with strength and the flesh on it with weakness.

----

28. Origen, Homilia prima on Exodus, PG 9, 227D.

29. HP vol. II, p. 81.

30. HP vol. I, p. 34.

31. HC PL 178, 155. PL 90, 288-296; 520-521.

32. Rev 21; Ezek 40-48; Isaiah 10.24; 12.6.

33. PL 178, 124-125.

As Abelard draws a moral from each saint he eulogizes, so there is a moral to be drawn from the examples of sin in human nature. Although he does not dwell on sin in general, but rather on the redeeming love of Christ, his hymn # 14, "Post prandium," describes the gluttony that must be avoided. The many biblical references in the hymns, like those in St. Bernard's sermons, are probably second nature after his years of biblical study. He nearly always interprets, expands, or symbolically explores the biblical passages used as a starting point. "I distinctly feel that it gives Abelard a definite pleasure to disguise many of the biblical reminiscences."[34]

Like his predecessors and contemporaries, Abelard involved himself in numbers as a means of symbolic interpretation, their fixity in the order of creation being an assurance of the immutability of God. The perfect number of six, divisible by two and three, whose elements of one, two, and three add to the total and also multiply to it, was the subject of his Hexaemeron. But he also deals with the number four, meaning in many cases the four Gospels, as in # 93.2. A window at St. Denis in Paris shows the ark of the covenant on four wheels which are the emblems of the four evangelists.

Liberal arts studies had long been divided into the quadrivium and the trivium, making the imperfect number seven, but Abelard uses the number especially for the seven gifts of the Holy Spirit in # 69 for Pentecost. The name of the feast underlines the fifty days from the resurrection, and recalls the Israelite jubilee when after fifty years the alienated territory must be restored.[35] The dedication hymn, # 74, explains its own use of numbers.

It is hard to tell what feeling Abelard had for nature, since he lived in an age entirely dependent on nature and came from an estate in the uncultivated west of Brittany. Gougaud refers to the "the large space allotted in [Celtic poetry] to scenes of nature,

----

34. HP vol. I, pp. 88-89.

35. Lev 25.8-17.

familiar or picturesque, and to animals."[36]   The
bestiaries, stemming from the older _Physiologus_, were
popular, taken from biblical sources as well as from
pagan, and from Gregory the Great in his _Expositio
super cantica canticorum_.[37] In Genesis Jacob blesses
his son saying, "Judah is a lion cub,"[38] to which
Abelard refers in hymns # 53-56.   St. Peter is the
shepherd, a theme recurring in medieval art.[39]   The
dove is the symbol of the Holy Spirit, used in the same
way in Abelard's Pentecostal hymns, # 36, 3.   St.
Bernard, in spite of what he thought were excesses in
Abelard, used "a rich ensemble of picturesque symbols
. . . from Pliny and the ancient naturalists through
the Fathers of the church, St. Isidore of Seville, and
the medieval bestiaries and lapidaries."[40]

Dom Jean Leclercq notes the term "philosophy" in
Abelard's century as holding different but related
meanings, namely, all wisdom, even of the pagans; but
when it was qualified as "true philosophy," it could
only mean the true religion, the divine philosophy,[41]
and this definition lasted.   An awareness of the
austere traditions of the eastern church "was an
important contributary factor in the formation of a new
climate of religious opinion in the Latin church, which
found expression in the spiritual centers of Camaldoli,
Citeaux, and the Charterhouse [Carthusians] in the 11th
and early 12th centuries."[42]

----

36. Louis Gougaud, _Christianity in Celtic Lands_ (London
    1932) p. 56.

37. Friedrich   Lauchert,   _Geschicte   des   Physiologus_
    (Geneva 1974).   Gregory, PL 79, 209, 475, 490, 511.

38. Gen 49.9.

39. Jn 21.15-17.   See Emile Mâle,   _Religious Art in
    France in the Thirteenth Century_, tr. Dora Nussey
    (Paris 1966), p. 17

40. Jean Leclercq, _St. Bernard et l'esprit cistercien_
    (Paris 1966), p. 17.

41. Leclercq, _Etudes_ pp. 51, 77.

42. Bernard Hamilton, _Monastic Reform, Catharism and
    the Crusades_ (London 1979), p. 212.

Abelard did not hesitate to differ from his teachers, questioning Augustine's phrase, "Crede ut intellegas Verbum Dei," --Believe, so that you may understand the Word of God-- and Anselm's "Fides quaerens intellectum" by saying "Intellego ut credam," --I understand, so that I may believe.[43] Abelard's opponents argued that logic is alien to faith and can harm faith; the second is admissible, but to Abelard to know truth can never be an evil, even when the subject is evil.[44]

Helen Waddell in her article on John of Salisbury says, "The quality in Abelard which distinguished him to John is the quality which has survived the summer lightnings of his fame; the solid honesty, humility even, of his intellectual purpose."[45] He was thought by his students to be the only one who could understand Aristotle. At a time when Gratian's Decretum was being formed, when the Investiture Conflict was at a high pitch, and the Crusades were moving all Europe, Abelard's concern was with definitions of theology. Like Gratian's canon law, it has long outlived other controversies.

----

43. Augustine, Sermon 43, PL 38, 257-258. Anselm, Proslogion, PL 158, 227 C.

44. Beonio, ed, The Logic of Abelard, (N.Y. 1970), p. 22.

45. Helen Waddell, "John of Salisbury," in Essays and Studies, The English Association, XIII, ed. C.E.E. Sturgess (Oxford 1928), pp. 28-51; see pp. 39-40.

The hymns in Migne's <u>Patrologia Latina</u>, volume 178, 1772-1818, number only ninety-three. Dr. Joseph Szöverffy in 1975 published his annotated text, including forty more hymns from a collation of the manuscripts from Brussels and Chaumont as well as from the edition of Dreves. His work has been critized by Peter Dronke and by M. Silvestre, and where it made a difference in translation I have followed Silvestre's corrections.

Dr. Szöverffy's introduction to the <u>Hymnarius Paraclitensis</u> (HP), volume 1, contains much material on Abelard's background and his skill both as poet and as liturgist. The collection of one hundred and thirty-three hymns is not · complete, for parts of the manuscript are missing. There are no Advent hymns, and though no hymn exists for St. Stephen, there are hymns for St. John the Evangelist and the Innocents at the same time of the year. Some of the apostles' days have no hymns, nor does the feast of the Trinity. Father Chrysogonus Waddell concludes in his analysis of the liturgy that the abbey of the Paraclete, for whom the hymns were written, adopted the Cistercian breviary, adding its own feasts.[1]

Abelard wrote for a Benedictine convent, partaking of Cistercian reform. The Office, the daily services, also called the Hours, are the main work of a contemplative house, for as the <u>Opus Dei</u> of Benedict's Rule, they constitute the corporate worship of a monastic family. "Let nothing be put before the Work of God."[2]

The first Office of the day, said before daylight, though contrary to the common notion it does not interrupt the night's sleep, is Matins, consisting of groups of psalms called nocturns, introduced by an unchanging canticle. Each nocturn begins with a hymn and continues with six psalms which change with the

----

1. Chrysogonus Waddell, "Peter Abelard as Creator of Liturgical Texts," paper read at Kalamazoo International Congress of Medieval Studies, 1975.

2. RB, ch. 43, "Nihil operi Dei praeponatur." PL 66, 215-930.

day, followed by responsory verses and a Bible reading. The next Office at daybreak is called Lauds because the last three psalms in the psalter, with which the Office invariably ends, begin with <u>Laudate</u>. These Offices are followed by the "Little Hours," the shorter Offices of Prime, Terce, Sext, and None, spaced at the first, third, sixth, and ninth hours of daylight; then Vespers before dark, and finally Compline to end the day. Since Matins, Lauds, and Vespers are the more important Offices, Abelard has for most of the days provided hymns for them only, three hymns for the three nocturns of Matins in one day, and one for Lauds and one for Vespers. For Sunday and for the greater days of Holy Week hymns are provided for all the Hours. All hymns in a given group are of the same meter to fit the available plainchant melody.

Hymns for specific saints are called "propers," and others called "commons" can be used for any saints. The term confessors refers to those willing to acknowledge Christ though not called on to give their lives.

A recent critique of translations said, "The passion of a translator is a form of intellectual generosity, and also love. He knows the riches that are there, and he wishes to make them available." In Fr. Chrysogonus' words, "Abelard's hymns teem with imagination, and the lofty standard of his poetic skill maintains iself stanza after stanza."[3] This gives a translator pause, for it is impossible to transpose the poetic skill of one language to another. The bonds of meter and rhyme prevent a literal translation, making compromise necessary. One can only try to grasp the main thought of a stanza and express as much of the other words as possible within that frame. The stanza belongs to the whole hymn, and the hymn to its setting in the liturgy as well as to Abelard's known thought, to be presented with Abelard's dignity and unquestioned devotion.

The English language because of its many consonants and monosyllables does not sound like Latin, and although Abelard uses little assonance and less

----

3. Chrysogonus Waddell, <u>St. Bernard and the Cisterican Office</u>. Paper given at the Kalamazoo Conference 1975, p. 33.

alliteration, the sound in poetry is important. He makes frequent use of cognate words, a form of repetition considered unsuitable in classical Latin but obviously deliberate in Abelard, a characteristic I have tried to carry out. Abelard was as exact in his choice and position of words as he was in meter.[4]

The translation of verse into English meters involves considerable adjustment. Even in prose, "translating the Latin of Abelard is a tricky task, and only those who have not tried their hand at it will be deceived by its apparent simplicity."[5] An author of this period deliberately neglected the rules of classical verse.[6] It is likely that the spoken language even of the classical period, in contrast to conscious art, was less observant of the length of syllables, making its point with pitch and volume.[7] Abelard's language had long departed from the rules of the Augustan period. The pressures of vernacular speech released the language from its formality and artificiality, although the church's continuous use preserved its identity. The result of the process was a purely syllabic poetry, building its line on a count of syllables rather than on the modern feet of contrasting stress. There were no iambs, trochees, or dactyls, but simply a certain number of syllables, exactly kept, to each line.[8]

This change of emphasis, to the even flow of unaccented lines, was the basis for the Gregorian chant. As metric music is different from the chant, so classical Latin poetry is different from the medieval. In a modern hymn the syllables are compressed or

----

4. Jean Jolivet, Arts du language et théologie chez Abélard (Paris 1969), p. 211.

5. Etienne Gilson, in preface to Muckle, p. 9.

6. Dag Norbert, Introduction à l'étude de la versification latine médiévale (Stockholm 1958), p. 106.

7. Helen Waddell, A Book of Medieval Latin for Schools (London 1954), preface.

8. W. Beare, Latin Verse and European Song, pp. 95-102.

stretched on a Procrustean bed; in the chant the stresses shift with voice rhythm. So it is with modern French poetry, and so it was with Abelard's.

Since our English speech does not flow so evenly, the question for the translator is to adjust each verse to one of the English feet. Iambic verse is perhaps the most common, as in Shakespeare's pentameters, and this appears in the first nine hymns of the translation. # 10 and the following hymns use a longer line of twelve syllables, and although they could be translated into iambs, I have followed the plan of Dr. J. M. Neale who put # 29 into lines of four dactyls catalectic, that is, with the unaccented syllables cut from the end.[9] The reader cannot help noting the variety of meters and Abelard's skill in combining them.

He uses the vocabulary of Christian Latin in which salus means salvation, sacramentum a mystery, virtus becomes moral virtue, and Greek words like baptizo are absorbed.[10] Abelard ignores the classical quantities of vowels in rhyming what would be long and short, gurgitis with tenebris.

The hymns were meant to be sung, for as Abelard said in his preface, no hymn could be a hymn without its music.[11] Foreseeing a difficulty for Eloise's nuns,

----

9. Hymnal 1940, # 589.

10. Christine Mohrmann, Liturgical Latin (Washington 1957)

11. HP vol. II, Libellus primus, p. 10.

he wrote some melodies himself, of which the only identifiable one is that associated with # 29, <u>O quanta, qualia</u>.

Stäblein, Bruno, <u>Monumenta Monodica Medii Aevi</u> (Kassel 1956), 1, 514.

Lorenz Weinrich considers it surprising that Abelard should have rejected all the words and music at the Paraclete when revision would have been possible, but

> as a theologian he contends that many texts are unsuitable; however, as a musician he holds that melodies were being transferred to completely different texts . . . What makes these songs interesting for us is their spiritual mode of thought and their new rhythms, qualities which were not particular-ly advantageous for their dissemination . . . Peter Abelard, a true artist, had a fine sensitivity for the relation of word and tone.[12]

An anonymous critic, himself a poet, has written:

> These poems mainly transcend the usual limitations of religious poetry; they achieve spirituality, the conviction of adoration. . . There is in many of them a complex, an intense poetic imagination . . .

----

12. Lorenz Weinrich, "Peter Abelard as Musician," in <u>Musical Quarterly</u>, 55, 1969, pp. 295-312, see pp. 300, 312.

Though he works with tight meters and rigid
schemes, Abelard often achieves excellent
conceits, extends metaphors brilliantly,
develops a long musical line . . . The
unique, the unusual, the slight (or not so
slight) off-centeredness, the authenticity of
the forms. . . He is a voice that would
suggest much of poetic possibilities to the
current ear . . . My own response to many of
these poems is the response of a surprised
and delighted discovery.

Abelard justified his life and all his teaching by
the statement he put at the end of the prologue of his
Sic et non: "In doubting we come to inquiry; by
inquiry we perceive the truth."[13] He had said of
himself in the Historia, "I reckoned myself the only
true philosopher left in the world,"[14] yet he also
said in a letter to Eloise, "I will not be a
philosopher if it means rejecting Paul. I will not be
an Aristotle if it means to be shut off from Christ."[15]

> Ou est la tres sage Hellois
> Pour qui fut chastré et puis moyne
> Pierre Esbaillart a Saint Denis?[16]

> Where's Héloise, the learned nun,
> For whose sake Abelard, I ween,
> Lost manhood and put priesthood on?[17]

----

13. PL 178, 1349.

14. PL 178, 126.

15. PL 178, 375.

16. N.P. Jannet, Oeuvres Complètes de Francois Villon
    (Paris 1870), p. 34.

17. William M. Rossetti, Poetical Works of Dante
    Gabriel Rossetti (Boston 1891), p. 237.

LIBELLUS PRIMUS

Abelard's First Preface

At the urging of your request, Eloise, my sister, dear once in the world and now dearer in Christ, I have composed what are called hymns in Greek and <u>tehillim</u> in Hebrew. Since you and those women of holy profession who live with you have often urged me to write them, I asked your will about it. I felt it would be unnecessary for me to produce new ones when you have quite enough of the old, and it would seem sacrilegious of me to put new songs of sinners before the ancient ones of the saints, or to emulate them. But when I had different answers from different people, you, I remember, added this among other things: "We know," you said, "that the Latin and especially the Gallican church hold to their own custom both in psalms and hymns rather than follow authority." We still consider it doubtful whose translation this is which ours, the Gallican church, uses. If we want to judge from the opinion of those who showed us the diversity of translations, it differs widely from the general interpretation, and will hold no weight of authority, I believe. The use of long custom now prevails, so that although we hold in other things to the passages corrected by blessed Jerome, in the psalter, which we use most, we follow unauthorized versions.

There is such confusion in the hymns that we are now using that few or none of the titles assign any hymn to anyone, and if certain authors, of whom Hilary and Ambrose are believed to be outstanding, then Prudentius and many others, seem to be attached to certain ones, the inequality of syllables is often such that the songs scarcely fit the melody. Without melody there can be no hymns, for their definition is the praise of God with music.[1] You add that for many feasts proper hymns are lacking, those of the Innocents and evangelists and of those women who as virgins and martyrs were less conspicuous.

You said then that there were some hymns, these among them, in which the singers had to improvise, as

----

1. Dr. Szöverffy quotes Augustine's comment on Psalm 48, "Laus ergo Dei in cantico hymnus dicitur." PL 36, 1948.

31

much for the necessity of the meter as for the inclusion of false notes. It may happen that the faithful, often caught in circumstances of this kind, either anticipate the fixed times of the Office or the Office anticipates them, so that they have to adjust even the time of the day, when, for example, they sing the night hymns in the daytime or the day hymns at night. They are determined not to be idle in the praise of God even at night, according to the authority of the prophets and the church's order, as it is written, "All night, Yahweh, I remember your name,"[2] and again, "I get up at midnight to thank you,"[3] that is, to praise you; and the other seven times of praise, of which the prophet also says, "Seven times daily I praise you;"[4] unless they be performed in the day. The first of these, which gets its name from the morning praises, about which it is written by the same prophet, "I meditate on you all night long,"[5] is to be offered in the very beginning of the day, when dawn or the morning star shows light, as it is expressed in many hymns. When it says,

Rising at night time, let us watch together,
and again,

We interrupt the night with song,
or,
We rise at night to praise the light
And break the bondage of the night,
or,
The night has spread its darkened wing
And steals the hue from everything,
or,
We rise from bed before the light,
The time of quiet in the night,
and,
As we awaking to prolong
The hours of the night with song,

----

2. Ps 119.55.

3. Ps 119.62.

4. Ibid., 164

5. Ps 63.6

and more of the same kind; these hymns witness of themselves that they are of the night. Thus morning hymns also and other hymns of a particular season often make clear their purpose by what they say, as when it is said,

> Shadows already now are slipping from us,

and again,

> See now, the daylight comes in gold,

and,

> The dawn has touched the heaven's height,

or,

> The dawn of light is glowing red;

and another is,

> The bird of morning tells of day,
> Approaching light as dark gives way,

and,

> The risen star of day is bright.

When they are of this kind, the hymns themselves instruct us at the time of singing, until, if we did not observe their proper times, we should be found false in their very rendition. It is not so much negligence that brings this observation for the most part, as that a certain necessity or circumstance hinders us, for especially in parishes and small churches the daily occupations of the people themselves, carried on entirely in the day, call for it. Not only does the wrong observation of the time produce falsehood, but even the composers of certain hymns, either considering other hymns in the uncertainty of their minds or wishing to praise the saints in the zeal of a thoughtless piety, have gone so far beyond measure in some things that against our own conscience we are offering things foreign to truth itself. There are few who are able to go on singing in a worthy manner while they weep and groan in the process of their contemplation or the remorse of their sins,

> We pour our prayer with sorrow's din;
> Release us, Lord, from former sin,

and again,

> Receive with kindly favor, Lord,
> The tears we shed with one accord,

and others like them, fitting for some, but those are
few. With what presumption have we not feared to sing
every year,

> Martin, the apostles' equal,

or to glorify certain confessors beyond measure for
their miracles, saying,

> Often have sick ones, coming to your graveside,
> Asking for health in poor and ailing members,
> Even oppressed and heavy with their burdens,
>   Found restoration,

it is in your judgment to decide. Because of these and
your similar arguments, my respect for your reverence
had compelled my spirit to write hymns for the whole
year. And so, as you, the brides and handmaids of
Christ, have asked me to do this, we too ask you in
turn to lighten with the hands of your prayers the
burden you have put on our shoulders, so that whoever
sows or whoever reaps, we may all rejoice in working
together.

     The subject of the first nine hymns, for the early
morning Office, is creation and man's praise of God,
befitting the early day. As in almost all the hymns of
the Hymnarius, each ends with a doxology, a stanza of
praise to the Trinity.

     Aelred, the Cistercian abbot of Riveaulx, wrote of
the six days of creation in his Speculum Caritatis.[6]
How closely nature and the Office could be associated
is well illustrated by Ambrose in his description of
the sea: "The chants of the singers compete with the
sound of the gently flowing waves; the islands rejoice
in the quiet chorus of the flow of the saints and
resound with the hymns of the saints."[7]

----

6. Compendium speculi caritatis, Corpus Christianorum,
   Continuatio medievalis, ch. xii, xiii, pp. 190-192.

7. J. Migne, Patrologia Latina, 14, 178: "...ut cum
   undarum leniter alluentium sono certant cantus
   psallentium, plaudant insulae tranquillo fluctuum
   sanctorum choro, hymnis sanctorum personent."

1   SUNDAY   Matins: first nocturn

1.
      Creator of the universe
      And of the whole creation nurse,
   The universe of your creation sings
   And you are praised in all created things.

2.
      You have no need of instruments
      Nor theories of excellence;
   Your word alone fulfils the promises.
   You say, "Let it be done," and so it is.

3.
      A builder most illustrious,
      Omnipotent, not envious;
   Whatever things therefore you mean to make
   Become the best their properties can take.

4.
      The judgment brought by such a one
      Will not condemn as evil done
   What man can take and put to common use.
   It cannot limit Godhead nor reduce.

5.
      The world is then made very good
      With all things joining as they should,
   In weight, in number, and in measurement,
   That order may not feel a detriment.

6.
      The work is worthy of his hand,
      In beauty and endurance grand,
   Perfection made to the Creator's mind,
   His image showing all things as designed.

7.
      Nor is the governance less wise
      Than was the founding enterprise.
   Whatever evil wickedness achieves
   The highest justice steadily retrieves.

8.
      Eternal glory must be his
      Who has determined all that is.
   To him from whom they are, let all things raise
   Their joy, their love, their everlasting praise.

2   SUNDAY   Matins: second nocturn

1.
      You teach us, Lord, your own intents
      From writings in the Testaments,
   And in the sweetness of the wisdom there,
   You put together songs of daily prayer.

35

2.   To you be it acceptable,
        For us it will be practical,
    That when we pay our praises to your name,
    We understand your undivided claim.

3.   The triune God's intelligence
        Will furnish varied condiments,
    The fertile table of the sacred books
    Abounds in new delights in taste and looks.

4.   The children feed on history
        Those more advanced on mystery.
    In hard pursuit of those who came before
    We learn salvation's lesson more and more.

5.   Our faith is built on mystery,
        And zeal produces fruitfully.
    The fruit's completion is what one believes
    And what direction in us life receives.

6.   We welcome, Lord, this nourishment,
        Prepared for us, your favor sent,
    That in unsettled living here below
    The pilgrim's food of grace may overflow.

7.   Eternal glory . . .

        # 3   SUNDAY   Matins: third nocturn

1.   To rise into the world of sense,
        The new-made world's intelligence,
    Now heaven and the earth were once complete,
    Proceeds from God the Father's holy seat.

2.   The heaven soon is set apart
        For angel citizens to chart.
    Forever praising their Creator's name
    The morning stars enkindle there their flame.

3.   The earth was lying void and still;
        The waters overflowed at will.
    The face of the abyss in swirling mud
    Was shadowed by the darkened cloud and flood.

36

4.   The warming Spirit quickening
         Has brooded on the waters' spring,
That in this place and that they should give
                                   birth
And bear a sacred offspring to the earth.

5.   The light is giving charm and grace
         To beautify the new world's face.
Said God, "Let there be light," and it was done.
Then shadows were divided from the sun.

6.   Eternal glory . . .

4   MONDAY   Matins

1.   The Lord from heaven's throne has stirred
         And said to his co-equal Word,
"Let firmament on earth be now imposed,
And let the higher waters be enclosed."

2.   The word is followed by the deed;
         Creation is from chaos freed.
The earthly waters now are held below,
And those suspended high are made to flow.

3.   The Lord alone discerns the use
         Of gathered waters he may loose,
But clearly all is brought to bear alone
On our delight, nor ever for his own.

4.   He gives for our necessity
         The whole of nature's treasury.
For every separate gift of God we owe
More thankfulness than any heart can show.

5.   Eternal glory . . .

5   TUESDAY   Matins

1.   The work of God in these three days
         Demands of us responsive praise.
The lower waters regulated here,
The Lord has covered earth with ocean's sphere.

2.   And earth once covered sings awake
      The grass and trees by sea and lake;
      Of grass the countless pollen heads are loosed;
      Of trees the countless saplings are produced.

3.   To rule this land the Lord will place
      Mankind, as man's productive race.
      He garnishes the earth with beauty's touch,
      And all to make our human living such.

4.   We should be cursed in everything
      Should we ignore creation's King,
      For he demands in us a reasoned base,
      The Lord who for us set all things in place.

5.   The world before us stands apart,
      Reworked for us with every art.
      May grace present to God our hearts and wills
      Unhampered to return the lives he fills.

6.   We give him pleasure with our praise,
      But lose him whom our sin betrays.
      What joy a sacrifice of praise may be
      The scriptures tell us in their psalmody.

7.   Eternal glory . . .

      # 6   WEDNESDAY   Matins

1.   New growth has covered earth in green,
      And now new lights in heaven are seen.
      With sun and moon and stars the sky is set,
      For whose good use creation is in debt.

2.   They separate the dark and light,
      The movements of time's pressing flight;
      For nature keeps in order all aspects
      Of planets and of lands and their effects.

3.   Remember, child of God, for you
      Was made the earth from which you grew;
      But heaven's country calls itself your own
      With all the functions nature here has grown.

4.   By sun alone can man be warm
      Who lacks the fire in winter's storm.
      The poor man in the darkness of the night
      Yet has the moon and stars for his delight.

5.   In bed of oak the rich man lies;
          The poor the meadow satisfies,
For here in melody the birds are spent;
And here each flower adds its separate scent.

6.   My friend, you spend your wealth too fast
          In building that which will not last.
You paint the ceiling with a sun on high
And fill with pictured stars the seeming sky.

7.   Below the roof of very sky
          The poor man sleeps in heaven's eye.
The very sun, the constellations there,
The Lord has painted as the poor man's share.

8.   More striking than the work of man
          Is nature's when she first began,
For she needs neither labor nor expense,
Nor is a death old age's consequence.

9.   The rich man's flattery is sure,
          But angels bend to help the poor.
So here the Lord's arrangement for us stands:
The heavenly things subjected to our hands.

10.   Eternal glory . . .

      # 7   THURSDAY   Matins

1.   The sky above the world now dressed
          In light, creation's loveliest,
There lies below, still unadorned, this home
To be illumined from that new-lit dome.

2.   The reptiles spawn within the seas,
          And thence come birds in companies.
At one effective sign both bird and fish
Have grown in form of their Creator's wish.

3.   The animals at sea grow great
          With smaller shell fish as their bait,
While in one instant griffins reach their height
And gentle sparrows gather to alight.

4.   He spoke the word and it was done;
        He gave command and made it one.
Both great and small receive their properties
From him who fashions both with equal ease.

5.   Eternal glory . . .

        # 8   FRIDAY   Matins

1.   The sixth day now demands its praise,
        The climax of the weekly phase;
For this day saw mankind itself appear
For whom creation looked in all the sphere.

2.   In this new light now shed on earth
        The living spirits have their birth.
The crawling beast of earth, from earth once
                                        torn,
Produces every race of creature born.

3.   But last of all mankind is made,
        To whom their deference is paid.
In him creation sees its final goal,
As if the end that makes creation whole.

4.   He is creation's highest form
        And of high works he is the norm.
In this accomplishment is all fulfilled;
The reasoned order shows what God had willed.

5.   In this one nobly moulded man
        There shines, O Lord, your total plan,
For he reflects the beauty of your face,
The glory, and the likeness of your grace.

6.   The man at first, then womankind
        Is from the rib of man refined.
The Lord had sent symbolic sleep on man
To mean the death from which her life began.

7.   The other forms of life to these
        Are given as heaven's sureties.
They reach the open gate of heaven too
In clothes of mortal flesh as nature grew.

8.   Eternal glory . . .

40

1.
    With all completed, that there lurk
    No weakness in his finished work
The Lord before his own creation stood
And joyed to see indeed that it was good.

2.
    Then six, the perfect number, saw
    The whole of chaos under law.
The strength of number in itself betrays
The perfect work in perfect length of days.

3.
    He rested on the seventh day,
    No less in power for the stay;
For God himself is rest perpetual;
In him our coming rest is mystical.

4.
    And so he sanctified the day
    In which the work's completion lay,
The symbol of our holy sabbath rest
For which the day forever shall be blessed,

5.
    That very sabbath day indeed
    Whence endless sabbaths yet proceed,
In which true peace from dissidence released
Has yoked all days in one eternal feast.

6.
    Eternal glory . . .

10 is the first of the hymns for the day Offices, which continue through # 17. Abelard has inserted the <u>post prandium</u> hymn after the midday meal. # 10 through 29 are composed of lines of twelve syllables that fall easily into dactylic meter, in which the rhyme is on the unaccented syllable.

10   SUNDAY   Lauds

1. Truth is returning and shadows are vanishing;
   After the darkness comes light with the day's new
                                                spring.
   Daylight now reddens the shine of the morning star,
   Lifting the shadows of law from the hearts afar.

2. Precepts of night time belong to Mosaic law;
   Day has its own refrain, new songs the mornings
                                                draw.
   Everything rises with Christ from his hiddenness.
   Never will such a light leave us in loneliness.

3. Mystical symbols now throw off all secrecy;
   Truth is apparent, no longer in mystery.
   Filling prophetic responses with ecstasy,
   Highest and deepest it penetrates searchingly.

4. Evening has meaning, as death in its dolefulness;
   Life is resurgent with dawn in its joyfulness.
   God has arisen, the angels are witnesses.
   Guards are in fear, for the splendor is luminous.

5. Saints who had slept through the ages of history
   Rising, proclaim the Lord's rising as verity.
   Proofs of the Lord in his rising are glorious;
   Mortals reach upward while angels descend to us.

6. Glory eternally be to the Trinity,
   All things from, in him, and through him in unity.
   All from the Father proceed through the Word,
                                                the Son,
   Held in the Spirit who makes the whole three in
                                                one.

1. The morning star precedes the dawn, then comes the
                                                   sun.
    By dawn is meant the light of faith where faith is
                                                   won.
    The light of truth in rising brought this kind of
                                                  dawn,
    When Christ had blossomed forth in flesh, his
                                          sorrows gone.

2. This morning star will shine as shines the sun,
                                              no less,
    When they together come to try our righteousness.
    His presence then will so illuminate our lives
    That consciences will speak the fault whence guilt
                                              derives.

3. The star we see is herald of the coming sun,
    The sun we know, whose progress has not yet begun.
    So does the unseen author of the things we see
    Receive the praise from us whom he has made to be.

4. O man, be no more silent in creation's praise,
    For you too owe the Lord the debt creation pays.
    Each separate benefit from him is ample cause
    For gratitude from hearts whose zeal allows no
                                              pause.

5. Eternal glory let there be from us to God,
    For all things come from him and through him at
                                            his nod.
    The Father is the source and works but through
                                            the Son;
    The Spirit of the two is love, to make them one.

             # 12   DAILY   Terce
          Adjusted meter   Dactylic   Catalectic

1. High in its orbit the sun has arisen;
    Heat with its health has reopened earth's prison.
    Light came before, then the heat is engendered.
    So is faith first, to which love has surrendered.

                            43

2. God is the true sun, the faith of the lover;
   Christ has accepted our flesh as his cover.
   Heaven itself is the gift at this hour,
   Spirit of love from the Lord in his power.

3. Rightly we recognize Spirit as burning;
   So on the Twelve it was fire of yearning.
   Love is a fire to light understanding,
   Strengthening brick with the heat of its banding.

4. Glory to God from the things he created,
   In whom and through whom are all things related
   Coming from God through the Son to restore us,
   Living in God and his Advocate for us.

13   DAILY   Sext   Adjusted meter

1. Full in the sky is the light of the sun;
   Full on the world has the heat overrun.
   Symbol of perfect beatitude this;
   God will enkindle a vision of bliss.

2. Can we acknowledge the sun in its might,
   So much the greater will be our delight,
   Looking at nothing but God in the sun,
   Joying in loveliness consciously won.

3. Blessed the vision and happy the eyes
   Given a glory that beatifies.
   We as your suppliants ask it, O Lord;
   Grant us the heavenly mansions' reward.

4. Glory eternally be to the Lord;
   All things from, in him, and through him accord.
   All from the Father proceeds through the Son,
   Held in the Spirit who makes the three one.

14   POST PRANDIUM
Adjusted meter   Ten syllables

1. God, who have made both the body and soul,
   Making by nourishing food a new whole,
   You we will give from both bodies and souls
   Praise for the life which their union extolls.

2. Pass over, Lord, our intemperate will,
   If beyond measure we fatten it still.
   Surely, most holy one, sins that we own,
   These like the others we pray you condone.

3. This was the exile our ancestors earned,
   Whence is the ill their descendants have learned.
   This is for us what our nature instilled:
   Faults that the parents to offspring have willed.

4. If we are feasting immoderately,
   If in our talking the reins are too free,
   This we appeal to your patience and heart:
   Out of your favors reserve us a part.

5. Yours is the graciousness answering prayer,
   Grant us restraint to preserve us aware.
   Yours is the wisdom to portion the mean,
   Ruling our nature, impatient and keen.

6. Wanderers here and enfeebled at length,
   Take away avarice, give us your strength.
   Thus will the burden of appetite yield,
   Lest we be driven from heaven unhealed.

7. Why as a sojourner pamper your taste?
   Empty you slip from the life you embraced,
   Empty the plank in a castaway's grip,
   Driven on rocks from the wreck of your ship.

8. He who is nourished on heavenly bread,
   Let him not go where the dung heap is spread.
   He who by spirit has fattened his soul
   Should not eat cake for his stomach's control.

9. He who is drunk on the true vine alone
   Takes no delight in a wine of his own.
   Favors of kings, and not Christ in his poor;
   These are the prizes the world will secure.

10. These make not heaven but earth their concern,
    Scorning the joy of an exile's return.
    These take the lot of the beasts as their own,
    Freely embracing what men should disown.

11. Eager to seek the descent into hell,
     Loth to ascend the hard path, they rebel.
     Crawling on stomach and face here below,
     All aspirations they hopeless forego.

12. Down on all fours in the form of a brute,
     Made so by gluttony, heavy and mute,
     Zealous in worship of love and of wine,
     Rash devotees of the stomach, they dine.

13. Lord, bring us back through a holy restraint,
     Exiles corrupted by gluttony's taint.
     Always your help to your people is sure,
     Clothing the lily and feeding the poor.

14. Let us not suffer hard pressure of need;
     Grant us good use of the bounty decreed.
     Thus may we harvest enough to suffice
     Comfort for nature and nothing for vice.

15. Glory eternally . . .

     # 15   DAILY   None   Adjusted meter

1.   Seven times daily we offer due prayer,
     Eight when the matins at night have a share.
     Give of them four to the setting sun's ray,
     Four of these early ascribe to the day.

2.   Noon we acknowledge as evening begun;
     Thence we conceive the decline of the sun.
     Otherwise justly a man may assign
     Dawn after midnight to wait the sun's shine.

3.   Eight are the ages completing the span,
     Symbol of height of perfection of man.
     Four are the elements, virtues as well,
     Pressing on man their demand to excel.

4.   So do we rightly in hours of praise
     Give to the Lord our assent in eight ways,
     Pleading the sins of the body at night,
     Offering vigor of soul in daylight.

5.   Glory eternally . . .

                        46

1. Eight are the ages we read in the psalms,
    Promising glory with victory's palms.
    Light on the faithful will endlessly rest
    After the seven are fully expressed.

2. Now we acknowledge the seventh fulfilled;
    Christ has arisen who Friday was killed.
    Blessed assurance he gives to his friends,
    Hope to his own whom as head he defends.

3. This for the Christian is rightly a day
    Kept as a feast beyond others' array.
    Endless the good, and no temporal lot
    Falls to the Christian whom God has begot.

4. Never in those who pursue the hard goal
    Reason that cowardice chills a good soul.
    This is the day when the Paraclete came
    Sent by the Lord as a spirit in flame.

5. Add for the glory of this holy day:
    This is the Lord's, under only his sway,
    For in humanity now was the Lord
    Welcomed as king and as royalty's ward.

6. Entering thence to his palace by right,
    Power he shows as a king in his might,
    Casting out wickedness, healing the blind.
    Thus is his house reconciled to his mind.

7. Jesus has finished the mystery's eight;
    Now he is seated to adjudicate,
    Lighting his friends by his presence alone,
    Casting out wickedness; his is the throne.

8. Nor as a mystery is it undone;
    Pagans have given this day to the sun.
    As in his name the significance lies,
    Also the sun in his justice shall rise.

9. Glory eternally . . .

1. Always and everywhere must we employ
    Praise and thanksgiving to tell you our joy.
    Places and times you create for our need;
    Working in daylight, at dark we are freed.

2. Only our weakness rejects a long day,
    Marks off its hours and limits their stay.
    Thus do these places prepare us for work,
    Using these times for the many who shirk.

3. Seven the hours of daylight complete,
    Rest in the evening our praises will greet.
    Bless us, O Lord, in our sabbath's demand.
    Peace may refresh us as sent by your hand.

4. Sanctify us and our home with your grace.
    Bind again sin's savage heat in its place.
    Freshen our bodies with peaceable rest.
    Hearts will awake, as our vigils attest.

5. Glory eternally . . .

18-29 are for the weekdays, for the principal Offices of Lauds and Vespers. Abelard carries three threads of symbolism: the ages of history, the age of a man, and the six days of creation, as mentioned in the Introduction.

18   MONDAY   Lauds   Adjusted Meter

1. God has prefigured our world and our time;
    To him the order of number is prime.
    Six as we read were creation's events;
    Six are the ages of human ascents.

2. Noah is set as the end of an age;
    Infancy's symbol, we count it a stage.
    Growing responses to objects appear.
    Nature's first day holds the mysteries here.

3. Then inchoate was the substance of earth,
    Still to be formed, nor selective of birth.
    Law was unknown to the world in its youth,
    Nor to the age did it signify truth.

4. Gone was this age when the flood had prevailed,
    Just as our childhood's remembrances failed.
    First on this morning the light was released;
    Earth in its infancy saw light increased.

5. Still for the incomplete faith has a light.
    We like the children accept it as right.
    Vision will show us the light to pursue
    When what we now believe opens as true.

6. Glory eternally . . .

19   MONDAY   Vespers   Adjusted meter

1. Abraham shows us the second divide;
    So when as boyhood is reached in a stride,
    Floods cannot wash it from memory's truth.
    Everyone knows the estate of his youth.

2. This is the day when the land was exposed,
    Holding the waters divided and closed.
    Thus had the ark from the deluge prepared
    Refuge by which the believers were spared.

49

3. Not as of yet were the people of God.
    Law of the scripture had not shown its rod.
    Nor did his manhood give fruit to the boy,
    Although remembrance had found its employ.

4. After the light of faith, hope gives us force,
    Stirs the believer to bravery's course,
    So that by hope of the heavenly joy
    All things are lifted from earthly alloy.

5. Glory eternally . . .

         # 20   TUESDAY   Lauds   Adjusted meter

1. Up to King David the third epoch ran.
    This corresponds to the youth of a man.
    Wisely interpreters, seeing this third,
    Judge it with those that already occurred.

2. Light has translated the seas from dry land.
    Law has forbidden unrighteous demand,
    Lest in oppressive unholy desire
    Man and his spirit be lost in his fire.

3. This is the age when the law brought to birth
    Abraham, father of thousands on earth.
    Then as the mortals on land reproduce,
    So with the lands are the trees for their use.

4. Glory eternally . . .

         # 21   TUESDAY   Vespers   Abelard's meter

1. After our faith and the hope it accompanies,
    Fear is the drive of the slave and of briberies.
    This one they press for reward as convenient,
    Others they rouse with their whips as a
                                        stimulant.

2. Thus it was fear which possessed the old Israel,
    Subject to threats of the law inescapable.
    Then while the law promised good to its
                                        followers,
    Punishment heavily fell on the wanderers.

3. Plants that we see as alive in fertility
   Fashioned today as we read in their history,
   These were for Israel's life in the countryside;
   Theirs was the promised land as it was prophesied.

4. Glory eternally be to the Trinity,
   All things from, in him, and through him in unity.
   All from the Father proceeds through the only Son,
   Held in the Spirit who makes the whole three in one.

   # 22   WEDNESDAY   Lauds   Adjusted Meter

1. Heaven the fourth day is girdled with stars;
   Fiery vigor the force it unbars,
   Never diminished, consuming as love,
   Claiming its right to the mansions above.

2. Gospellers' law is divided four ways:
   Four corresponds to the number of days.
   Strength in a four-sided block is immense;
   Love unsubdued is creation's defence.

3. Love is achievement of virtue's increase,
   Strong and mature in perfection of peace,
   Filling humanity's body with strength;
   So will love consummate wisdom at length.

4. Glory eternally be to the Lord . . .

   # 23 WEDNESDAY   Vespers   Adjusted Meter

1. Teachers of doctrine put David's command
   Fourth in the burgeoning age of the land.
   That epoch's evening saw Israel's host
   Driven in exile to Babylon's coast.

2. Love in King David we know was complete,
   Mastering rage and accepting deceit.
   Saul he reprieved and lamented in death;
   So died the lie with the messenger's breath.

3. Love overpasses the plunderer's hate,
    Nor will the soul be subdued to its fate.
    Where love is lacking salvation is lost;
    Then the heart's citadel suffers the cost.

4. Glory eternally . . .

    # 24   THURSDAY   Lauds   Adjusted Meter

1. This is the fifth of the ages of earth,
    Brought by tradition to Christ at his birth.
    Man to renew the decline of the age
    Enters anew his regenerate stage.

2. Age in a man suffers loss of his force;
    So of the world in senility's course.
    Whence the Most High sent his grace to direct
    Growth of all good from our mortal defect.

3. Now patriarchal devotion had passed;
    Prophets had failed, and the seers were outcast,
    When the anointed one came full of grace
    Who in the Spirit restores his embrace.

4. Glory eternally . . .

    # 25 THURSDAY   Vespers   Adjusted Meter

1. Truths of the scripture in teaching agree
    Life on this day was produced from the sea.
    Baptism's font was a place yet to come,
    Whereof the old dispensation was dumb.

2. Now has the new mother buried the old;
    Hereafter Christians receive a new mold.
    John gives the sacrament, heralding first
    Christ in his baptism, wholly immersed.

3. Here in the fifth of these ages is sent
    Him who will open the fifth day's intent;
    End of the old, giving new water's grace,
    So he might make us a life-giving race.

4. Glory eternally . . .

26   FRIDAY   Lauds   Adjusted Meter

1. Sixth of the ages of man, as of earth,
   This is completion and goal of its worth.
   Christ is the goal of perfection and good,
   Suffering ill from the world he withstood.

2. His is the suffering, ours is the rest,
   Good in completion, contentment unguessed.
   Fruitlessly man to salvation aspires;
   This is the victim salvation requires.

3. Born on this day, man has squandered his right;
   Christ on the same day restored him to light,
   Then, by accepting the gallows, disgraced,
   Ransomed the slave from the sin he erased.

4. Woman is made from the sleeping man's side;
   Christ has exalted the church as his bride.
   Death is for Christ his creative repose;
   Blood with the water for cleansing us flows.[8]

5. Glory eternally . . .

27   FRIDAY   Vespers   Adjusted Meter

1. Image we say of a person or thing
   Must have exactness of feature to bring.
   What on the other hand actions express
   Cannot pierce fully the external dress.

2. God has set man over woman, we know.
   His was the bodily flesh to bestow.
   Hence is he image of God, we assert;
   Woman the likeness, a picture inert.

3. Whence is the greater dominion of man,
   Passing in power the feminine span.
   Man and the Godhead can interrelate;
   Reason yet gives to the woman her state.

4. Glory eternally . . .

----

8. This stanza is shifted by Fr. Chrysogonus from # 27.

28   SATURDAY   Lauds   Adjusted Meter

1. Rest and enjoyment is labor's reward,
   Now as love's gift to the blest of the Lord.
   This is the meaning in passing of hours;
   Six are the days of creation's new powers.

2. Faith; and a holy fear; hope; and delight;
   Grace of baptizing; Christ's death in its
                                          might.
   Six are the graces and six are the days
   Which in their loveliness shepherd our ways.

3. Step after single step lead us, O Lord,
   Members to head of the body restored.
   Then in the true sabbath's glory at last
   Joy in the Lord will transfigure the past.

4. Glory eternally . . .

29 SATURDAY   Vespers   Adjusted Meter

1. Great are the sabbaths, enduring and deep,
   Those that the heavenly courtiers keep,
   Those that rest weariness, those praising
                                          strength;
   God will be all in all, welcome at length.

2. There is Jerusalem, vision of peace,
   City whose honors forever increase.
   There is no search for desire unfound,
   Nor is desire's fulfilment uncrowned.

3. How great the king and his court where they
                                          dwell!
   How great the rest and the peace they foretell!
   Let them describe what a joy they possess
   If what they feel they can justly express.

4. Ours it is meanwhile to point our desire
   There to the country to which we aspire,
   Then to Jerusalem turning at last
   Homeward from Babylon, no more outcast.

5. Soon our distresses will plague us no more.
   Verses to Sion the songs that we pour,
   Thankfulness always for gifts of your grace,
   Lord,we bring up to you, we of your race.

6. There to a sabbath the sabbaths succeed;
   Joy in the Lord makes a sabbath indeed.
   Never an end to the hymns will there be,
   Sounding a melody, angels and we.

7. Glory eternally . . .

LIBELLUS ALTER

Abelard's Second Preface

The Office of divine worship is in three parts.
The teacher of the nations in his letter to the
Ephesians ordered them, "Do not drug youselves with
wine; this is simply dissipation; be filled with the
Spirit. Sing the words and tunes of the psalms and
hymns when you are together, and go on singing and
chanting to the Lord in your hearts."[1] And again he
says to the Colossians, "Let the message of Christ, in
all its richness, find a home with you. Teach each
other, and advise each other in all wisdom. With
gratitude in your hearts sing psalms and hymns and
inspired songs to God."[2] The psalms and canticles,
since they have been prepared in ancient times from the
canonical scriptures, should not lack our interest or
anyone's, if only they can be put in order.

Since nothing in the above scripture quotations is
expressly about the hymns, although some psalms have
the name of hymns or holy canticles written in their
titles, it was written in afterward indiscriminately,
and proper hymns were given for variety in seasons and
hours or for some festivals, and these we now properly
call hymns, although formerly some called whatever
canticles of divine praise were composed in rhythm and
meter hymns and psalms. Eusebius of Caesarea in the
seventeenth chapter of the second book of his
Ecclesiastical History, recalling the praise of the
eloquent Philo the Jew for the church at Alexandria
under Mark, adds among other things, "After a few other
things he wrote again about how they make new psalms,
saying thus they not only know the hymns of fine
writers of the past, but they themselves are making new
hymns for God, composing them in all meters and tones
in quite dignified and smooth combinations." It is
perhaps not at all unsuitable that all psalms made in
the Hebrew rhythm or meter and set to pleasant music
should be called hymns, according to that same
definition of hymns which we placed in the first
preface. But since now the psalms have been translated

----

1. Eph 5.18-19.

2. Col 3.16.

57

from the Hebrew into another language and are freed from the laws of rhythm and meter, the apostle writing to the Ephesians, who are Greek, does well to distinguish hymns from psalms, and canticles too.

Since you have urged our small skill, dear daughters of Christ, with many requests, adding further the causes which seem to you to make it necessary, now as far as the Lord allows, we have partly obeyed your request. We have included the daily hymns of ferias in the former book, which we believe can suffice for the whole week. You know that these were so composed that they are in two parts as far as tune and rhythm go, and there is one common melody for all the nocturns and another for the day hours to go with the rhythm. We did not omit a hymn of thanksgiving at the end of a meal, according to what is written in the Gospel, "After psalms had been sung, they went out."[3]

Others of the above hymns we have formed with this consideration, that those for the night should contain the work of their own weekdays, but the day hymns should handle the allegorical or moral interpretation of their work. So it is that the darkness of history will be kept for the night, but the light of explanation for the day. I ask only that I be aided by your prayers, so that I may hand over to you this little work you wished.[4]

----

3. Mt 26.30.

4. Abelard drops into the first person singular in place of the more formal plural he had used above.

The Christmas hymns, # 30-33, emphasize the poverty of Christ's birth and reflect the new interest in the humanity of the Lord.

30   CHRISTMAS   Matins: first nocturn
Iambic meter; ten syllables

1. By word of God the maiden bears the Word.
   The sun is rising from itself, the Sun.
   By him illumined, light itself widespread
   Has shaken out the clouds and daylight won.

2. O welcome day, the glory of all days,
   Whose rising sees these joys for mortals won.
   O welcome mother, who has born her God;
   O welcome star, who bore the very Sun!

3. How lovely is this poor-born pregnancy,
   Whose term enriches every king who reigns.
   Poor-born indeed, but sprung from heaven itself,
   The blood of kings and priests within her veins.

4. Along the way the Way of life she bore;
   A shelter but no home she found that day.
   Offspring of kings and heaven's lady too,
   For lady's chamber found the stable's hay.

5. No nurses in this labor took a part,
   But angels were her aid in labor's hour
   Who in their numbers instantly fold wing,
   Whose coming spoke the joy of godly power.

6. No bath perhaps was offered to her there,
   But she whom it would cleanse would show no spot.
   No pain presaged this childbirth so conceived,
   Nor wounds defaced his birth, the Unbegot.

7. In height of heaven glory be to God
   And covenant of peace to us on earth.
   The very angels serving at her feet
   Have sung today this maiden and this birth.

31 CHRISTMAS   Matins: second nocturn
Abelard's meter; ten syllables

1. Only son of father's and mother's will
Cradles humbly, resting on manger-fill,
Bears the manger's narrow encirclement,
He for whom the heavens are pediment.

2. He accepts the shed by the stable wall,
He who rules the heavenly palace hall.
Who believes it? Who is not stupefied?
Where the soul not moved to subdue its pride?

3. God is helpless, none without help as he.
Thus he willed it, born for us willingly.
How receive it, how can we welcome it?
What return to God has a like merit?

4. Cradled poorly, child-like he cries aloud,
He who lightens heaven's dark thunder cloud.
Straw and hay are his for his infancy,
He who grants the purple to royalty.

5. Laid is he in fodder for coverlet,
Bread of angels, lying in mortal debt.
Beasts surround him there in close company;
Here the angels worship his majesty.

6. Glory be to God in his holiness,
Peace on earth in contract of righteousness.
Over all the angels respond to us,
Knowing earth today to be glorious.

32 CHRISTMAS   Matins: third nocturn and
Vespers; Abelard's meter

1. Blest is bedding shed by the meadow beast,
Pressing close on her whose constraint has
ceased.
Here the child is found in his swathing bands,
He who holds the heaven within his hands.

2. Queens in silk and royalty's coloring
Share the mother's pain in her child-bearing.
Lying so in bedding of poverty,
Nothing can he know of anxiety.

60

3. Nourishment of kings to satiety
    Flows from her, his nurse's fecundity.
    Here he thrives on food from a maiden breast,
    Food she gives with maidenhood unpossessed.

4. Not to kings for all their high banqueting,
    All their tables' various surfeiting,
    Nor was granted to their posterity
    Thus to grow on milk of virginity.

5. Poor and thirsting, hungering possibly,
    Still she gave the milk for his infancy.
    Heaven marvels, angels are wondering;
    With his milk he mingles their worshiping.

6. Glory be to God in his holiness . . .

    # 33   CHRISTMAS   Lauds   Abelard's meter
                                Ten syllables

1. O maiden, glory of maidenhood,
    Mother too, rejoice for all motherhood.
    You alone were worthy to bring to us
    Joy for saints, redemptive and generous.

2. Sprung from kings and patriarchs worthily,
    God has promised you as the progeny.
    Symbols found in law have prefigured you;
    Prophets sang your praise to the chosen few.

3. You they seek who speak to you faithfully;
    All our hearts are turned to you mightily.
    You alone are hope in the Lord for us,
    Advocate, solicitor glorious.

4. To the judge's mother together go
    Those the judge's anger will overthrow.
    Well they know for such she will supplicate;
    She as sinners' mother is dedicate.

5. Holy mother; Son for our holiness;
    Thus she bore him, thus he was born to bless.
    So her slaves through grace are regenerate,
    Grace that this day shows to be very great.

6. Glory be to God in his holiness . . .

34-37 are concerned with the Epiphany. # 34.2 refers to an incident related by Paulus Orosius in his Seven Books of History Against the Pagans, in which a crown around the sun was visible and oil flowed from a fountain. In stanza 4 Orosius tells us that Augustus refused to be called lord.[5] This bears a resemblance to Vergil's Fourth Eclogue which eulogizes the child to be born and was taken by Christian writers to refer to Christ.[6]

34   EPIPHANY   Matins: first nocturn
This follows Abelard's rhyme scheme of an inner
rhyme in the first and third lines and an end
rhyme on the second and fourth lines.

1. Now preparing or appearing,
      King of heaven as of earth,
    With a token surely spoken
      Tell they worthily this birth.

2. For, Augustus, when you ruled us
      Came a crown around the sun.
    Oil was flowing, clearly showing
      Where the altar's stream had run.

3. The Redeemer came as Savior;
      Freedom for the slaves was won.
    You will waken the downtrodden
      And, unknowing, preach the Son.

4. You were never by your order
      Called a master by your own,
    So that only Christ can rightly
      Claim the honor of the throne.

5. Christ has given peace from heaven,
      Holding fast the gates of war.
    Prophets' sayings give the meanings
      Promised to the world before.

----

5. PL 31, 1053, 1058.

6. Vergil, Eclogues, Loeb Classical Library; Ec. IV,
   pp. 28-33.

6. Peace to mortals, peace to angels,
     Highest glory where they soar.
    To the Father, the Redeemer,
     To the Spirit evermore.

   # 35   EPIPHANY   Matins: second nocturn

1. Shepherds hearing angels' warning
     Wonder at the distant song.
    Star in heaven moves the wise men;
     Herod's fear contrives his wrong.

2. Orders gives he, all too harshly,
     Speaking to them but in guile.
    So the traitor is the loser,
     Each deceived by other's wile.

3. But they wisely hold their journey,
     Finding what they sought before,
    And they offer three-fold treasure
     To acclaim him they adore.

4. But returning they have warning
     Not to follow Herod's course,
    And instructed, are directed
     Henceforth by a heavenly source.

5. Peace to mortals, peace to angels . . .

   # 36   EPIPHANY   Matins: third nocturn

1. Into water blessed with power,
     There baptized by John his friend,
    Goes the Savior for the sinner,
     Having nothing to amend.

2. This baptizer with his power
     Gives baptism real and true.
    Then the curtained heaven opened,
     Closed before to sinners' view.

3. Then unclouded there descended
     God the Spirit as a dove,
    In baptizing re-ascending,
     Proving present grace thereof.

                    63

4. Then the Father's voice delivers
   Commendation for the Son.
   Those are really sons who duly
   Are reborn by graces won.

5. Bird of whiteness as of meekness [7]
   Shows us God as reconciled,
   Nor does any type so fully
   Tell his character as mild.

6. Peace to mortals, peace to angels . . .

   # 37   EPIPHANY   Lauds

1. Sanctifying waters flowing
   By his own baptismal rite,
   He will offer wine from water,
   Fill the guests with new delight.

2. Whence the festal day is able
   Splendidly to shine in light.
   So salvation to us given
   Through these signs is known aright.

3. Not for finer nor for greater
   Signs will yet the Jew believe,
   Though Chaldaeans' computations
   Find the star they can retrieve.

4. All the fire, earth, and water
   Recognize their final source;
   Miracles nor law and honor
   Move you, sinner, from your course.

5. If no wonders nor the seers
   Are to be relied upon,
   By a foreign master stricken
   Know yourself the guilty one.

6. Peace to mortals, peace to angels . . .

----

7. Mk 1.10

38   THE PRESENTATION OF CHRIST IN THE TEMPLE
Matins: first nocturn   Abelard's meter
Luke 2.22-38

1. Prepare, O Sion, bridals now
    To meet the Lord in marriage vow.
    Receive the bride and bridegroom's choir
    With light of waxen candles' fire.

2. O prudent virgins, watching late,
    Adjust your lamps equipped to wait,
    And let the young attendants rise
    And run to where their mistress cries.

3. Let servants light the torches' flame
    And for that light that this time came
    To light the world, let all the place
    With all within make bright his face.

4. O blessed ancient man, make haste!
    The promised joy is here embraced.
    Reveal to all in humble guise
    The light to lighten Gentiles' eyes.

5. Devoted widow, consecrate
    To God and to his temple's gate,
    Speak too with your prophetic joy
    Your honor in the Lord's employ.

6. To God the Father with the Son
    And with the Spirit ever one,
    As one in substance are the three,
    So also may one glory be.

39   THE PRESENTATION OF CHRIST IN THE TEMPLE
Matins: second nocturn

1. His parents bring the Christ to grace
    The temple in the temple's place.
    He willed to keep the law, although
    The law was made for man below.

2. Present, my lady, this your boy,
    The Father's and your only joy.
    Present him who presents us too,
    The prince who brought us back anew.

3. O maiden of the heavenly King,
    Present your Son as offering.
    Symbolic birds are now prepared,
    The sacrifice you both have shared.

4. The pigeon shows your single mind,
    The dove, a virgin long designed.
    This little victim may be poor,
    But great the mystery and sure.

5. Although among the poor indeed,
    The rich man's lamb has come to bleed.[8]
    And here the very lamb is seen,
    The mystic lamb the symbols mean.

6. To God the Father . . .

   # 40   THE PRESENTATION OF CHRIST IN THE TEMPLE
                 Matins: third nocturn

1. Who recommends true poverty
    Shows it himself for all to see,
    And God whose riches all are sure
    To make us rich became most poor.

2. In deed he showed what was within,
    And then he taught his discipline,
    And even from his childhood bed
    Made clear in action all he said.

3. The flaxen rope is here defined,[9]
    The cord the angel's hand entwined;
    The fine-spun word of Gospel law
    Is woven into act with awe.

4. And here the reed of measurement
    The child holds as his instrument
    To measure out the builder's site
    Established on the mountain height.

----

8. 2 Sam 12.1-4.

9. Ezekiel 40.2-5.

66

5. The book of Gospels is the reed,
   A yardstick for our use indeed,
   Which he is said to take in hand
   Who has fulfilled the book's command.

6. The church is measured by this reed
   As if by it to judge her creed.
   So each in measuring perceives
   How far he fails and what achieves.

7. To God the Father . . .

41 THE PRESENTATION OF CHRIST IN THE TEMPLE
Lauds

1. Let every male and female sing
   Of every age, the joy they bring;
   For he incites us all to joy
   Who comes with hope without alloy.

2. Sing man, and woman, sing as well;
   A common joy we have to tell,
   For all unknown to man she bore
   Mankind, which God in manhood wore.

3. Let maid's with maiden's joys accord,
   For this is mother of the Lord.
   Let wife to wife in love agree,
   Who tells what soon the child will be.

4. Enclosed within the womb as yet,
   The infant with rejoicing met
   The world's new life, and as was due
   Informed the world of what he knew.

5. The old man came, the widow came,
   To praise with prophet's zeal his name.
   Acknowledging his presence then
   They showed him Lord and Christ to men.

6. To God the Father . . .

42-44 for Good Friday have been put into Abelard's own meter, with the rhyme on the unaccented syllable. In these as in the Holy Saturday hymns which follow he uses four-line rhymes, easier to do in Latin than in English because of case endings. It is noteworthy that what would be long and short vowels in classical Latin are here of the same length, as in lacrimis and sceleris; and the -ae ending is the same sound as -e, so that Domine and gloriae rhyme. Tau, the Hebrew letter, indicates the cross in medieval symbolism.

55-56 for Holy Saturday refer to Genesis 49.9, the passage in which Jacob in old age foretells the lives of his sons and speaks of the lion of the tribe of Judah. This and the phoenix are taken from the Latin bestiaries.

42   GOOD FRIDAY   Matins: first nocturn

1. This is the night, brothers, night full of
                                    tearfulness,
    Wherein the light is confounded by gloominess,
    Full of the weeping of loyal devotedness;
    Crime and its magnitude force our resentfulness.

2. Traitor tonight is betrayed by himself alone;
    Feeding with sheep, as a wolf he is too well
                                    known.
    Christ is the lamb whom the wolf now has
                                    overthrown;
    Christ becomes cure for what crimes he will yet
                                    atone.

3. Christ while he offers the mystical sacrifice
    Sends his betrayer to practice a greater vice.
    Wicked accomplices give him his wicked price,
    So that the fee for the world will indeed
                                    suffice.

4. Lord, make us worthy to share in your sufferings,
    So be partakers in all that your glory brings.
    Here you are present in three days of evil
                                    things;
    We too will watch till the laughter of Easter
                                    rings.

43   GOOD FRIDAY   Matins: second nocturn

1. Trader in everything, Judas, what foolishness
   Sold your own life for the price of his holiness?
   Lest the transaction should add to your avarice,
   You will precede him in death in your wickedness.

2. So the betrayed be acknowledged in charity,
   Gives he a kiss as the mark of his perfidy.
   Wickedness mingles the name of his dignity
   Thus with the false salutation of treachery.

3. Held is the Lord in the bonds of his servitors,
   Loosening slaves from the cords of sin's
   creditors;
   Handed as guilty to guilty justiciars,
   He is the first and the wisest of lawmakers.

4. Lord, make us worthy . . .

44   GOOD FRIDAY   Matins: third nocturn

1. Lonely, O Lord, do you go to your burial;
   Thus for earth's death you have made yourself
   liable.
   What can we say to you, sinful and pitiful,
   We for whose failings they made you accountable?

2. Ours were the sins, Master, we are perfidious;
   You take the punishment, we are but ruinous.
   Let our hearts suffer in all that you do for us;
   Make us by grace of compassion as virtuous.

3. Three days of dark are a grief with us presently.
   Here where these sorrows are fixed let the
   evening be.
   Then will the dawn of your grace return joyfully,
   When the Lord risen will meet us eternally.

4. Lord, make us worthy . . .

45   GOOD FRIDAY   Lauds   Adjusted meter

1. Savior of all of us, Lord, whom we call
   King and especially priest for us all,
   Under a falsifed judgment you fall,
   Annas' and Caiaphas' high-priestly hall.

69

2. Made to be sport, you have suffered it long;
   Spitting you know, and the blows of the thong.
   Blinding your eyes, they redoubled the wrong.
   "Prophet," they clamor, "whose blow was so
                                       strong?"

3. Who of the faithful will not shut his ears?
   Who of mankind will not weep as he hears?
   Who sees this outrage without shedding tears?
   Whom does this madness not stifle with fears?

4. Lord, make us worthy to share in your pain,
   Thus have a part in the joy of your reign.
   Present in grief while the long hours wane,
   So may we laugh with the joy we regain.

46 GOOD FRIDAY Prime Adjusted meter

1. Judged before Pilate now, Lord, must you plead,
   Dragged as a spectacle, culprit decreed.
   Crown from the thorn bush and sceptre of reed,
   Purple regalia, mock while you bleed.

2. Mobs in their cruelty, innocence lone,
   Soften the pagan himself on the throne.
   Flogging as kinder than death he has shown,
   So their abusiveness be overthrown.

3. Forced to deliver you up to their spite,
   Keen to escape from what evil he might,
   Vainly he washes his hands in their sight,
   Cleansed from the blood of the just by this rite.

4. Lord, make us worthy to share in your pain . . .

47 GOOD FRIDAY Terce Adjusted meter

1. This is the third of the hours of day.
   Now has the rabble been granted its way.
   Shouts for the cross must the ruler obey.
   Bearing the cross, on the cross Christ is prey.

2. Therefore the Lord is on Calvary's brow,
   Known for the slaughter of criminals now.
   Bitter and mocking the cup they allow,
   Stripping him naked to hang on the bough.

3. Lord, make us worthy to share in your pain . . .

48   GOOD FRIDAY   Sext   Adjusted meter

1. At the sixth hour the cross was upraised.
    Darkness encompassed the sun that once blazed.
    Nature, to cover its sight as it gazed,
    Knowing its wrong to its sun, stood amazed.

2. While on the cross does the true Sun expire,
    With him the natural sun is on fire,
    Branding the crime of humanity dire,
    Showing how shadows and error conspire.

3. Lord, make us worthy to share in your pain . . .

49   GOOD FRIDAY   None   Adjusted meter

1. Now the true light in the ninth hour dies;
    Mankind receives again light it denies,
    Favor returned to the world as a prize,
    Pledge to the people it now terrifies.

2. Daylight returning, man listens intent;
    Earth itself moves at the ghastly event.
    Straightway the veil of the temple is rent,
    Sleepers from tombs have become evident.

3. Lord, make us worthy to share in your pain . . .

50   GOOD FRIDAY   Vespers   Adjusted meter

1. Evening; the cross has relinquished its Lord,
    Wrapped in the spices their customs afford.
    Loving regard has been tenderly poured;
    All their concern is to him they adored.

2. Now is the sepulchre sealed with a stone,
    Closed by the faith and the love of his own;
    Thus is the entrance kept hid and unknown,
    Till with his rising he burst it alone.

3. Nor does the Lord receive glory the less
    Though they set watches of evil duress.
    Conquered iniquity learns to repress
    Blasphemy's tongue by its power to bless.

4. Either the guards should return us our dead,
   Thus to receive the reward, as was said,
   Or in confessing them greatly misled,
   Tell our own joy in salvation widespread.

5. Lord, make us worthy to share in your pain. . .

51   GOOD FRIDAY   Compline   Adjusted meter

1. Woman whose guard at the tomb first began
   Yields not at all to the yielding of man.
   Fearless she looks on the might of the ban,
   Facing the threatening swords in the van.

2. For us the shepherd has suffered the blow,
   Losing the rams in his own overthrow;
   Love moderates what the sheep undergo,
   Casting out fear and absorbing its woe.

3. Lord, make us worthy to share in your pain. . .

52   HOLY SATURDAY   Matins   Adjusted meter

1. Since on the sixth day mankind had been made,
   Now on the seventh creation is stayed.
   History full of its treasures arrayed
   Foreshadows joy, and our fear is allayed.

2. Yesterday's holiness suffered defeat;
   Then our redemption was rendered complete.
   So, "It is finished," we too can repeat,
   Word of the Lord in its mystery sweet.

3. So much of agony finally past,
   Wherein the devil by God was outcast,
   Set is the stone of his bedchamber fast;
   There will the sepulchre rest him at last.

4. This you prepared for him, Joseph, when dead,
   Building your own and our tomb in his stead.
   Here you have given him earth for his bed,
   Resting in heaven yourself whom he led.

5. Lord, make us worthy to share in your pain . . .

53 HOLY SATURDAY   Lauds   Adjusted meter

1. Through these three days has the lion's cub
                                        slept.
    So say the prophets whose word we accept.
    Roused by the lion whose life he has kept,
    Out from the tomb on the third day he stepped.

2. Thus too the phoenix is strange and unique,
    Rising the third day resilient and sleek;
    No less of Christ do its mysteries speak,
    Wherein our own resurrection we seek.

3. Then after death she resumes her own look,
    Growing the feathers whose burden she shook,
    Spurning the weakness her wings cannot brook,
    Rising with Christ in the passage he took.

4. She unaware of the difference of sex
    Lives on unique as her nature directs,
    Filled with the Lord in her new life's effects,
    Stands over all in her nature's aspects.

5. Lord, make us worthy to share in your pain . . .

54 HOLY SATURDAY   Prime   Adjusted meter

1. Who will bait Judah's young lion at rest?
    Jacob, who asked it, knows now in his breast.
    Although he longs for it, he had not guessed
    How with a miracle he will be blessed.

2. Thus does the lion ascend to the prey,
    Still in the sleep of the tomb where he lay,
    Out of the wolf's power taking away
    Souls of the dead with their bodies today.

3. Lord, make us worthy to share in your pain . . .

55 HOLY SATURDAY   Terce   Adjusted meter

1. As the young lion went up to the kill,
    So went the Lord to the cross of free will.
    Dying for us, he had yet to fulfil
    All of the number in Tartarus still.

73

2. Now when the lion has taken the prize,
    Safely at rest with his plunder he lies;
    So was the Lord in their sorrowing eyes
    Rested in burial till he should rise.

3. Lord, make us worthy to share in your pain . . .

56 HOLY SATURDAY   Sext   Adjusted meter

1. Still as if sleeping, the young lion waits;
    Soon comes the time when his vigil abates.
    Death for the Lord and his sleep are but states;
    Quickly the one to the other translates.

2. Sleep is the stream in the way where he fed;
    This we remember the psalmist has said.[10]
    Lord, you drink death in the chalice instead,
    Whence resurrection will lift up your head.

3. Lord, make us worthy to share in your pain . . .

57   HOLY SATURDAY   None   Adjusted meter

1. Not of its nature but heaven's good grace
    Christ found a river where none had a place.
    He who knew nothing dishonored or base
    Could not feel pain looking death in the face.

2. This cup of death which the devil has poured
    Comes as our due for offenses deplored.
    Know then Goliath bereft of his sword,
    Killed by our David, the type of the Lord.

3. Lord, make us worthy to share in your pain . . .

      # 58-61 are devoted to Easter. In # 60 Abelard
uses Old Testament figures as symbols of the Lord:
Pharaoh drowning in the sea is the enemy, from Exodus
23-28; Samson is the Lord in his superhuman strength,
from Judges 14-16; and David dances before the Ark in
Sion, from 2 Samuel 6.14. These hymns are unusual in
that the refrain is in the second line.

----

10. Ps 110, Jerusalem Bible

58   EASTER   Matins: first nocturn

1.   Christian people, clap your hands;
        Risen is the Lord today.
        Death and Satan lie in bands,
          Christ in mastery.
        Run to where the victor stands,
          He who sets us free.

2.   Now the devil is undone;
        Risen is the Lord today.
        Hell despoiled and glory won,
          Christ led out his own.
        Angels crowded with the Son
          Upward to his throne.

3.   All the devil's guile has failed;
        Risen is the Lord today.
        Satan in attacking quailed,
          Seeing him in flesh
        Holiness at once unveiled
          Conquered hell afresh.

4.   Those below are now enslaved;
        Risen is the Lord today.
        Those above have all they craved.
          Heaven cries aloud.
        Hymns and psalms proclaim them saved,
          Earth is justly proud.

5.   Glory to the Father, for
        Risen is the Lord today.
        Triumph that the victor bore
          To our Lord is due,
        Equal honor evermore
          For the Spirit too.

59   EASTER   Matins: second nocturn and Vespers

1.   Give to Miriam the drum
        Risen is the Lord today.
        With her singing let her come
          To the Hebrews' throng.
        Let not Jacob render dumb
          Sacrifice with song.

2.   Binding Egypt mightily,
        Risen is the Lord today.
        God has made his people free
          But in flooded graves
        Overcomes the enemy
          In the Red Sea's waves.

3.   Let the melodist resound,
        Risen is the Lord today.
        She, the other Mary, found
          Truth, not only name;
        Risen body, clothes unwound;
          Hers the first acclaim.

4.   Let her sing more sweetly yet,
        Risen is the Lord today.
        Let her faithful friends abet
          Mingled song and prayer.
        So when the disciples met
          She had joy to share.

5.   Glory to the Father . . .

60   EASTER   Matins: third nocturn and Vespers

1.   Avarice is overthrown;
        Risen is the Lord today.
        Here the sword is Pharaoh's own,
          Killing him at sea,
        Where he perished all alone;
          Satan's type is he.

2.   Sion with her daughters chants
        Risen is the Lord today,
        Meets our David's sacred dance,
          Adding melody,
        Welcoming his bright advance,
          Victor's victory.

3.   This is Samson strong anew;
        Risen is the Lord today.
        Fenced about, his power grew,
          Opened hostile gates,
        Till the foreign nation knew
          Ruin in its fates.

76

4.   As the lion's progeny.
           Risen is the Lord today,
           Which the father hardily
            Wakes at three days' end,
           Following the victory
            Nature's rites attend.

5.   Glory to the Father. . .

61   EASTER   Lauds and Vespers

1.   In the gracious time of spring
           Risen is the Lord today,
           When the world began to sing,
            Nature to revive.
           Then the world's creative king
            Should return alive.

2.   All things are rejoicing now,
           Risen is the Lord today.
           Leaves appear on every bough,
            Grass is springing green.
           Odors, colors, sun allow
            Flowers to be seen.

3.   Winter now is yielding fast,
           Risen is the Lord today.
           Life that will forever last
            Is the priceless gain,
      Conscious now of nothing past,
            Sorrow, grief, or pain.

4.   So he might restore our light,
           Risen is the Lord today.
           Earth has felt the new delight,
            Sensing joy's accord,
           And to make her welcome bright,
            Blossoms with the Lord.

5.   Glory to the Father. . .

62   ASCENSION   Matins: first nocturn and Vespers

1.   He leaping over mountain heights
        On hills and valleys now alights,
      Calls the bride from mountain and hill country,
      "Rise, my sister, follow and come with me."

2. His father's palace comes to greet
   The heir who seeks his father's seat.
   Maidens cry out, "Hasten, my heart's delight;
   Sit beside me, here on the Father's right."

3. They watch, for your return is due.
   The Father's kingdom waits for you.
   With the Father, courtiers eagerly
   Seek your presence, answering joyfully.

4. What royal brides assembled wait,
   What queens attend your royal state!
   These you clothe in gold and embroidery,
   Purple robes emblazoned in jewelry.

5. To Christ on high be glory due,
   Who rising to the stars anew
   With the Father, one with the Paraclete,
   Rules the heights and depths from his mercy seat.

63 ASCENSION   Matins: second nocturn and Vespers

1. With bounding leaps of triumph won,
   The Father's own eternal Son
   Came to earth from heavenly palaces,
   Hell despoiled, its treasure he ravishes.

2. He issued from the Father's breast;
   In mother's womb he was possessed.
   From the cross he came to the sepulchre
   We are victors through him, the vanquisher.

3. They saw him go to heaven's height;
   A cloud received him, filled with light.
   Hands uplifted, so he was lost to them,
   Blessing those who stood at his mantle's hem.

4. To those who saw his bright ascent,
   And marvelled with their eyes intent,
   Angels stood beside them in charity,
   Fair in face and garmented splendidly.

5. "Why look with such astonishment,"
   They ask, "at heaven's firmament?
   Him you see departing in majesty
   So will come to judge with finality."

6. To Christ on high. . .

78

64   ASCENSION   Matins: third nocturn and Vespers

1. The church in faith espoused to Christ
   While still on earth her vow sufficed
   Calling daily, her he admonishes,
   Urging mind and heart to his purposes.

2. And let her answer, "Draw me, Lord,
   Stretch out your hand and bind the cord."
   Flying up on wings of the thunder cloud,
   Who can follow, lacking what you endowed?

3. Then let her ask for wings of doves,
   That she may reach the peace she loves;
   Sturdy feathers lining the eagle wing,
   These she uses, strong in the upward swing.

4. With wings, he gives the eagle's eyes,
   Whose steady gaze unmoving tries
   Rays of brilliance, urgent to repossess
   Heaven now, perfection of blessedness.

5. For living souls with eagle wings
   This place of heavenly gatherings
   Sanctifies the merits of holiness;
   Theirs are wings of God-given eagerness.

6. To Christ on high. . .

65   ASCENSION   Lauds

1. The Lord ascended heavenward,
   And all the lowest depths were stirred.
   Christ in triumph rises in majesty.
   Where the victor is, there will the rescued be.

2. The holy city of the king
   Leads out processions triumphing.
   "Welcome," sing the angels in gratitude,
   Then, "Hosanna," answer the souls renewed.

3. To these as if in eagerness
   And wonder none could yet express,
   Some replying now and again to us
   Soothe and gladden, singing their message thus:

79

4. "Is this the king of glory then?
   And what the victory for men?
   Who from Edom, coming in majesty,
   Clothed with purple, shines with intensity?"

5. "The Lord in strength and might it is,
   And triumph over hell is his.
   Strong in hand and mighty in victory,
   Now returns with Satan in slavery."

6. To Christ on high. . .

66-68 are sections of a hymn for the feast of the Finding of the Cross by Queen Helena, mother of the Emperor Constantine, some time before her death in 327 A.D. She used some scientific skill to locate the three crosses on Golgotha and to determine which was the Lord's.[11] This division of what may have been one long hymn is taken from Migne's Patrologia Latina, but Dr. Szövérffy printed another arrangement which produces five shorter hymns, to which Abelard refers in the third preface.[12] The third lines rhyme throughout the poems.

\# 66   FINDING OF THE CROSS   Matins: first and second
                                             nocturns and Vespers

1.   Welcome, our sovereign
     Standard from heaven,
       Welcome, most holy.

2.   Cross where the robber,
     Robbed of his plunder,
       Pays back the death fee.

3.   Gates of Avernus
     Lie now amorphous,
       Broken the door key.

4.   Tau is the letter
     Signed on the sinner,
       Blessing him fully.

5.   Wrath of the evil
     Murderous devil
       Lies in bonds tightly.

----

11. Eusebius, Vita Constantini, 3, 41, 44, tells of Queen Helena's good deeds but does not know this story. PG 13, 460-461: "mulier singulari prudentia," "mater religiosissima;" "Pauperibus autem ac nudis et omni spe ac solatio destitutis quamplurima donavit;" "pietatem erga Deum minime neglexit... in ecclesiam ventitabat." See also F. Horthausen, Cynewulf's Elena (Heidelberg 1936). Rufinus, Historia Ecclesiastica, PL 21, 467-540; see 476, 477.

12. Sz. vol. II, p. 170; also his note on p. 141.

6. Once you were torment
   Only for ill-spent
   Lives lived unjustly;

7. Now highly vaunted,
   Kings on their forehead
   Press the seal freely.

8. Life-giving timber,
   Whereon the Savior
   Mounted his palm tree;

9. He by this fruitage
   Counters the damage
   Left in the fruit tree.

10. Blessed the sailor
    Who with this anchor
    Finds life is happy;

11. Through the great ocean
    Man reaches heaven,
    Sailing securely.

12. Praise to the Father,
    Spirit and Savior,
    Trinal conjointly.[13]

67   FINDING OF THE CROSS   Matins: third nocturn

1. This is the serpent,
   Healing, as God meant,
   Casting out poison;

2. Cure of the ancient
   Tooth of the serpent:
   Christ's crucifixion.

3. Patriarch's wisdom
   Sees of itself come
   Sure medication.

4. Striking on flint-stone,
   Moses brought unknown
   Water's effusion.

----

13. The doxology is supplied from <u>Personis trino</u> . . .
    which is all that is given in the Latin text.

5. Christ on two wooden
   Crossbeams was smitten;
   He is our potion.

6. Jews are his people;
   Christians, immortal,
   Drink of salvation.

7. Praise to the Father. . .

68   FINDING OF THE CROSS   Lauds

1. Placed in the water,
   Sweetening bitter,
   Wood heals it safely.

2. Every submission
   Through crucifixion
   Sweetens the holy.

3. Noblest of willows,
   Drink of death's sorrows;
   His for us freely.

4. All of his torture
   Favors his own poor,
   Tracing his copy.

5. There is no sorrow
   Like to my sorrow;
   True testimony.

6. Yet he who carries
   All our vagaries
   Knows no vagary.

7. For all he suffered;
   All we, delivered,
   Suffer in pity.

8. Praise to the Father. . .

69-70 are the hymns for Whitsunday or Pentecost, the first of which gives one stanza for each of the seven gifts of the Holy Spirit, as listed in Isaiah 11.2-3: <u>spiritus sapientiae, et intellectus, spiritus consilii, et fortitudinis, spiritus scientiae, et pietatis, et replebit eum spiritus timoris Domini.</u>

70 begins with a reference to the fiftieth year of Jubilee, from Leviticus 25.11: <u>Iubileus est et quinquagesimus annus</u>; and Numbers 36.4: <u>Cum Iubileus, id est quinquagesimus annus, remissionis advenerit.</u>
71 contrasts the terror of the Old Testament appearances of God with the new arrival of the Holy Spirit. # 72 recalls the account of the first Pentecost, from Acts 2.1-36.

This hymn, # 69, shifts the meter within the stanza, but every stanza is the same.

69   PENTECOST   Matins: first nocturn

1.   The Holy Spirit comes to share
        His burning altar in our heart.
        Accept, O God, your temples there;
        With virtues dedicate their art.
     These are the sevenfold gifts you as God possess,[14]
        Binding seven demons of wickedness.
        These your gifts are goodness and holiness.

2.   The <u>fear</u> of God can set us free,
        But wickedness must first abate.
        The poor on earth with such a key
        May enter rich in heaven's gate.
     You, Master, give us this; give to us graciously.
        Give the guilty less than the penalty.
        Yours the glory, yours be the victory.

3.   And give us force of <u>holiness</u>;
        Let not temptation overwhelm.
        The mild and merciful possess
        This grace and all the earthly realm.
     And, Master, give us this. . .

----

14. The refrain for stanzas 1 and 9 is different from
    that of the other stanzas.

4.   Let <u>knowledge</u> fall on us as well,
        Through which we know the grace of tears.
        Your pardon casts its holy spell
        When we have paid up all arrears.
    And, Master, give us this. . .

5.   With holy <u>might</u> your strength is shed
        On those who thirst for rightousness.
        The fulness of the very bread
        Is vigor pilgrim souls express.
    And, Master, give us this. . .

6.   And give us highest <u>counsel</u>, Lord;
        Hereto your mercy will suffice.
        So may you then allow reward;
        For this you ask, not sacrifice.
    And, Master, give us this. . .

7.   In <u>understanding</u> you are known
        As God within the Trinity.
        The pure in heart can see alone
        The kingdom's high sublimity.
    And, Master, give us this. . .

8.   You give us <u>wisdom</u> finally,
        In which the sons of God take rest.
        The name of father makes them free
        To sanctify what there is blest.
    And, Master, give us this. . .

9.   By force of the apostles' prayers
        Whom you renewed at Pentecost,
        Give us the graces such as theirs,
        And strengthen us lest we be lost.
    These are the sevenfold gifts you as God possess,
        Binding seven demons of wickedness.
        These your gifts are goodness and holiness.

1.   The number of release of debt
        These fifty days have signified.
        The year of jubilee has set
        The contract's binding force aside.
    To God on high, the King, the highest glory be;
        His grace has made us worthy to be free.
        From him, through him, in him all things agree.

2.   And with this number of the days
        The Spirit of forgiveness came.
        The Son who sent him he obeys,
        As from the holy Father's name.
    To God on high. . .

3.   The Spirit, holy and divine,
        We give by right the name of love,
        Who to the sinner is benign,
        Who has the softness of the dove.
    To God on high. . .

4.   The flame of love today had birth
        And set the world itself on fire,
        For Christ has come to send on earth
        This flame his love and works require.
    To God on high. . .

5.   It hangs in fiery tongues today
        Above the twelve apostles' heads,
        To point the law its fiery way,
        These prophets of the light it spreads.
    To God on high. . .

6.   The ancient law in cold disgrace
        Coerced its slaves as with the rod;
        In Christ the mother full of grace
        Has born them truly sons to God.
    To God on high. . .

7.   By force of the apostles' prayers
        Whom you renewed at Pentecost,
        Give us the graces such as theirs,
        And strengthen us lest we be lost.
    To God on high. . .

1.   When God was giving men the law,
        The trembling mountain moved in dread.
        The faithful in assembly saw
        The Spirit lift it from their head.
     To God on high. . .

2.   The lightning there appeared in storms,
        The steamy mountain darkening.
        But here was flame in kindly forms,
        Not burning but illumining.
     To God on high. . .

3.   The frightful sound of trumpet blast
        Had struck the people to the ground.
        A new discernment came at last;
        The Spirit's voice was in the sound.
     To God on high. . .

4.   The smoke was in the mount to name
        The knowledge there but still obscure.
        They here receive the splendid flame,
        The very sign of knowledge sure.
     To God on high. . .

5.   With terror and with dark and heat
        Are all things filled that happen there.
        From opposites the Paraclete
        Can bring his opposites to bear.
     To God on high. . .

6.   The consolation he imparts
        Diverts our burdens graciously.
        He scores the tablets of our hearts
        With reason always as his plea.
     To God on high. . .

7.   By force of the apostles' prayers . . .

1.   To enter the apostles' breast
        The Holy Spirit comes to teach.
        He gives their hearts to wisdom's test,
        Their tongues to every nation's speech.
    To God on high. . .

2.   As once he shattered nations' pride
        By sharp divisions of the word,
        So now the humble are allied;
        All tongues resolved in one are heard.
    To God on high. . .

3.   To praise him all the tongues combine,
        And every voice must preach his name
        Who made this world by his design
        In all its parts and all its frame.
    To God on high. . .

4.   Of Joel's witness now we know
        This is fulfilment and defense,
        Which Peter used to overthrow
        The clamor of malevolence.
    To God on high. . .

5.   Of all the feasts of month and year
        The festivals have now been traced.
        In these his graces promised here
        The Lord's perfection be embraced.
    To God on high. . .

6.   The Spirit here is promised us
        To bring to mind what we have heard,
        For Christ the Son has spoken thus
        Who teaches truth in every word.
    To God on high. . .

7.   By force of the apostles' prayers. . .

\# 73-76 are for the festival of the dedication of
the church, in which the doxology is the same in all
four hymns but another stanza is also repeated in all
but the Lauds hymn. In \# 73.2 the words <u>basilica</u> and
<u>basileon</u> are examples of the common use of cognates in
Abelard's poetry. Here he refers to the Greek term
originally for the civic hall which had come to mean a
church, and he connects it with the word for king. \#
74 and 75 describe the ritual for the dedication;
stanza 12 recalls the story of the prophet Elisha and
his deceitful servant in 2 Kings 5, and Simon Magus
from Acts 8.18-24.

\# 73   DEDICATION OF THE CHURCH   Matins: first nocturn

1.   Once the dedication rite
     Filled Jerusalem anew,
     Since the Lord was present light,
     Focus of their earthly view.

2.   May he so assist today
     In our festival, we ask,
     Of the present kingdom's sway
     King himself, to bless the task.

3.   May he hallow for his own
     Temples in our willing breast,
     So by outward signs well known,
     Guide the flock to inner rest.

4.   What is given outwardly
     May he yet fulfil within,
     He who lives in secrecy,
     In the heart devoid of sin.

5.   To our God and Father be
     Equal glory with the Son;
     To the Spirit equally
     Render thanks for mercies won.

1. Sign and symbol of the Lord
   Is the temple here we see.
   In it all for us is stored,
   Yet remains a mystery.

2. Water by its blessing purged,
   Salt is mixed for sacrifice.
   With them is the church asperged,
   Carried in its circuit thrice.

3. Meanwhile are the lamps alight
   For the liturgy within;
   Twelve in number, making bright
   Circles where the rites begin.

4. Thrice the bishop moves around,
   Sprinkling all the temple floor.
   Thrice he makes his staff resound,
   Striking on the upper door.

5. Then he gives the needed word:
   Bring the King of glory in!
   When three times it has been heard,
   Doors are open to begin.

6. Entered to the church's throne,
   Prayers he offers to the Lord,
   Makes the sacrifice his own,
   Then that mankind be restored.

7. While he traces line by line
   All the double alphabet,[15]
   He has formed the holy sign
   Where the crossing lines have met.

8. What is given outwardly. . .

9. To our God and Father be. . .

----

15. Dr. Szövérffy notes the tradition of the ashes
    spread on the church floor in the shape of a cross;
    the bishop writes the Greek and Latin alphabet in
    the lines of the cross.

1. To the altar comes the priest
   Ready for the sacrifice.
   Mingled salt and water there
   With the ash and earth suffice.

2. Thrice does his anointed hand
   Touch the altar's sacred horns,
   Draws the symbol of the cross
   Hallowing what it adorns.

3. Then the prelate bearing high
   Hyssop on asperging reeds
   Round the altar seven times,
   Purges it for human needs.

4. Three times then within the walls,
   Sprinkled in the sacred rite,
   Does he pray the Lord to hear
   Those whose prayers he would unite.

5. At the altar once again,
   When his action here is done,
   Has the bishop turned to hear
   Psalm and antiphon begun.

6. At the altar's base is poured
   What of water now remains;
   Whitened linen then is laid
   On the stone made free of stains.

7. Incense then the bishop burns
   For the altar of the Lord,
   Signs the corners with the cross
   As the holy oil is poured.

8. Unction of the chrism oil
   All around the altar flows,
   With the holy antiphon
   Skilful chanters interpose.

9. Crosses with the oil are drawn,
   Twelve in number, on the wall;
   Covered is the altar well;
   Sacrifice is made for all.

10. What is given outwardly. . .

11. To our God and Father be. . .

76   DEDICATION OF THE CHURCH   Lauds

1. See the dwelling of the Lord,
   Look on it with fearful hearts.
   Psalms and hymns and holy songs
   Represent what faith imparts.

2. Let the Lord whose house it is
   Oversee it for his flock.
   Who as shepherd knows his sheep
   Builds their fold upon the rock.

3. May he give his watchful care
   To the faithful dogs on guard,
   Keeping wolves of evil will
   Shut away and safely barred.

4. Keeping watch with angels' ranks,
   Perfect in their loyalty,
   For the faithful people here
   May he set a guarantee.

5. Michael stands as warrior,[16]
   Grinding down the devil's pride.
   Let the healer Raphael
   Give the aid his skills provide.

6. Those whose hearts are faltering
   Gabriel can fortify,
   Standing in abiding strength,
   Fostered in his watchful eye.

----

16. Michael and Gabriel appear in the book of Daniel,
    8-10, and Raphael in the story of Tobit, all as
    archangels.

7. Never should this royal hall,
   Palace of the King of kings,
   Stand bereft of ministers,
   Sheltered by archangels' wings.

8. These are ministers who hold
   All things in a solemn trust;
   They who know the will of God,
   What is false and what is just.

9. Let the people of the Lord
   For themselves make vows and prayers.
   Let each show what things he asks,
   And what sacrifice he swears.

10. Not with empty useless prayers,
    Not with vows devoid of worth,
    Should a Christian pray for self
    Or for anyone on earth.

11. May the worshipers who here
    Raise their prayer for God to bless
    Finally rejoice to know
    What they sought for they possess.

12. Never let Gehazi here,
    Let not Simon with his plea,
    Bruise the faithful flock of Christ
    With the plague of heresy.

13. Those whom Christ himself expelled,
    Holding office wrongly bought,
    Let not man in pride restore,
    Lest in anger he be caught.

14. To our God and Father be. . .

LIBELLUS TERTIUS

Abelard's Third Preface

In the last two prefaces we prepared the daily weekday hymns and those proper to festivals. Now it remains that we should, as well as we are able, honor also the very court of the palace on high with worthy celebrations of hymns for the glory of the King of heaven and for the encouragement of all the faithful. In this task may they themselves especially help me with their merits whose benefits of glorious memory and of manifold praises I wish to repay, as it is written, "The virtuous man is remembered with blessings,"[1] and again, "Let us praise illustrious men."[2]

I beg you also, dear Sisters dedicated to Christ, at whose request I have begun this work, add the devotion of your prayers, mindful of the blessed lawgiver who accomplished more than the people could, by praying rather than by fighting.[3] And that I may find[4] your charity generous in the force of your prayers, think carefully how abundantly your intercession can benefit our ability. While we try to follow the praises of divine grace with our little skill, we compensate with the large number of hymns for what is lacking in the beauty of eloquence, namely, in composing proper hymns for the separate nocturns of the separate feasts, for only one hymn heretofore introduced the nocturns on festivals, as on ferias.

We have arranged four hymns for this reason for each festival, so that the proper hymn may be sung in each of the three nocturns, and its own hymn will not be lacking to morning Lauds. From these four we have

----

1. Proverbs 10.7.

2. Ecclesiasticus 44.1.

3. Moses.

4. Abelard here uses the first person singular, instead of plural.

ordered it that two be joined together for one hymn on the vigil,[5] and the other two be sung in the same way at Vespers on the festival day itself; or else that they be divided two by two in the separate Vespers Offices so that one be sung with the two psalms before it and the other with the two remaining psalms.[6] However, I remember that five hymns are written about the cross, of which the first should be put before the separate Hours, asking the deacon to lift the cross from the altar and bring it to the middle of the choir and to place it there as if for worship and reverence, so that in its presence the whole ceremony may be carried out throughout the day.

77   FEASTS OF ST. MARY   Matins: first and
                                   second nocturns

1. God, and Word of Godhead,
    Son, with God equated,
    Wisdom born of Father,
    Born, but not of matter,

2. Through whom we were fashioned,
    Through whom saved and quickened,
    Bend to hear your people,
    Supplicant and humble.

3. Judge and Master righteous,
    Christ, have mercy on us.
    Overlook our sinning,
    Good and just in judging.

4. Be for us a mortal,
    For us sacrificial,
    Giving hope of heaven
    For us doubly proven.

5. Be your birth not wasted;
    May no loss be counted,
    Nor may Satan scorn us,
    Trusting in your goodness.

----

5. The day before a festival is kept as a fast or vigil, but Vespers of the vigil is a festival Office.

6. RB ch. 17 prescribes four psalms at Vespers.

6. To the one and trinal
    Be our praise eternal.
    All things from and through him
    Were created in him.

78   FEASTS OF ST. MARY   Continuation of the above

1. Mother of all mercy,
    Hear us mercifully,
    Lest by false presuming
    Hope be self-deceiving.

2. Through you God's anointed
    To us has descended.
    Through you then ascending,
    We too look for healing.

3. Through you make us worthy,
    We who give you glory.
    Be his gate of heaven,
    Way for us to union.

4. To the one and trinal. . .

79   FEASTS OF ST. MARY   Matins: third nocturn

1. Mother of salvation,
    Think on your distinction.
    Weigh the name maternal,
    Great and honorable.

2. Bring to life the title,
    Though without the struggle.
    Knowledge of your pity
    Will involve the guilty.

3. With a mother's sanction
    May you ask protection.
    From your own son's patience
    Will you gain indulgence.

4. Such a son will never
    Hurt his holy mother,
    Nor your prayers' compassion
    Bring repudiation.

5. Holiness and virtue,
   Power given to you,
   Will obtain the favor,
   Be it whatsoever.

6. He will not hold worthless
   All his mother's kindness,
   Whose commandments honor
   Mother just as father.

7. To the one and trinal. . .

80   FEASTS OF ST. MARY   Lauds

1. Mother unexampled,
   Virgin still protected,
   God knows you as mother;
   To you comes the sinner.

2. Calling you in sadness,
   Sighing for your mildness,
   We attend your mercies
   In uncertain crises.

3. You are in a manner
   To the world a debtor.
   We as if in justice
   Claim with you a hospice.

4. You yourself so gracious
   Treasured this much for us:
   You as gate of heaven
   Counter Eve as fallen.

5. Once for this created,
   Then by grace elected,
   Call to mind the mission;
   Fill it in perfection.

6. Man claims your resources;
   Man returns your praises.
   After God, our solace,
   Ask of God his promise.

7. To the one and trinal. . .

98

81-84 are hymns for the feasts of angels, with more emphasis on the praise of God than on the angels themselves. This is characteristic of Abelard, who turns every good back to the God whence it came, as in the saints' hymns which follow. In # 81, the word laus, praise, in some form is found in each stanza. We see his careful structure here and his liking for symmetry in angelorum hominum; tam rector quam conditor; illi sursum, hi deorsum; coeli summa, terra ima; nullum tempus, nullus locus; and regna regit. # 82-84 speak of the warfare between Michael and his angels against Satan in the book of the Revelation 12.7-9; and # 82 of the parable of the woman with ten coins in Luke 15.8-10. # 84 translates the name Michael into Quis ut Deus?, "Who is like God?" In his Sic et non[7] Abelard describes the angels with quotations from Ambrose, Jerome, Isidore, and Augustine.

81   FEASTS OF THE ANGELS   Matins: first nocturn

1. Angels' God and man's Creator,
     Guardian of land and sea,
   As director, so as builder
     Of whatever things there be;
   Lost the very thing man lives by
     If unapt in praise is he.

2. Those the higher, we the lower,
     Let us chorus eucharists.
   Height above us, earth beneath us,
     Join the heavenly liturgists,
   Till no part of all earth's voices
     Stands aside where praise exists.

3. No one moment, no one movement
     Be bereft of righteous praise
   To the maker whose heart interest
     Never ceases nor betrays,
   But from whatsoever evils
     Fashions good from our essays.

----

7. PL 178, 1412-1417.

4. From and through and in him all things
   Give to him the majesty,
   Him whose kingdom rules unending
   Kings and kingdoms equally.
   For his coming all the ages
   Wait in high expectancy.

82   FEASTS OF THE ANGELS   Matins: second nocturn

1. Christ has told of ten new pieces,
   Money which a woman kept;
   One she lost, but nine remaining
   Even in the room she swept.
   So the blessed are distinguished;
   Fallen spirits we except.

2. Nine is given as the number
   For the angels in due course.
   For the filling of the places
   Holy scripture is the source.
   Nor did Satan, henceforth fallen,
   Keep his servers in his force.

3. These are lost indeed to heaven,
   Like the coin the woman lost.
   God will even seek the hundredth
   With all means he can exhaust.
   He, good shepherd, wants to carry
   Back his sheep at any cost.

4. From and through. . .

83   FEASTS OF THE ANGELS   Matins: third nocturn

1. O how favored are the armies
   In the heavenly column's van!
   They are serving as commander
   God of hosts in heaven's plan;
   Fighting in the strength of angels,
   Michael is the guardian.

2. While he fights the hostile dragon,
   War in heaven too is made.
   May the dragon, driven downward,
   Meet what he can not evade.
   Then the song of high thanksgiving
   To the Lord of hosts be paid:

100

3. "Now is come salvation, virtue,
   Kingdom and authority
Of our God and his anointed.
   Stricken is iniquity,
Which for long has been accusing
   Our own brothers ceaselessly."

4. From and through. . .

84   FEASTS OF THE ANGELS   Lauds

1. Who like God? and in his virtue
   Claiming power as in name,
Soldier of the Lord and sturdy,
   Architect of Satan's shame,
Trampling on the swelling dragon,
   Speared him in his jaws aflame.

2. We who ask the help of Michael,
   Valiant soldier for our part,
We whom this same adversary
   Still attacks with every art,
God, our hope and our salvation,
   Beg his arm may not depart.

3. When he fights thus stoutly for us,
   May the devil yield him place;
May he go with all his fellows,
   Vicious retinue and base.
Then let quiet souls imbue us,
   Let our hearts rejoice in grace.

4. From and through. . .

85-88 are "commons" for apostles, to be used for the feast of any apostle. # 87 and 88 point to the superiority of Christian simplicity over the pagan philosophy.

85   FEASTS OF APOSTLES   Matins: first nocturn

1. Christ as head of apostles' company
   Recreates us in joyful harmony,
   Yearly cherishing this festivity.

2. Standard bearers ecclesiastical,
   These are leaders in wars celestial,
   These present to us martyrs laudable.

3. Saints of other kinds as the infantry
   Bound to fasting with strong tenacity
   Lack no less in the Lord's own registry.

4. Lasting glory be given lastingly
   Here to Christ as the prince of chivalry,
   There to Father and Spirit equally.

86   FEASTS OF APOSTLES   Matins: second nocturn

1. Praise is due the apostles' faithfulness.
   All the world can partake of holiness;
   Through them God can be known in
                              righteousness.

2. Only Israel honored heretofore
   God's great name and creation's chancellor;
   Now they bring it to every auditor.

3. They for this were endowed with languages.
   Bright with miracles, they were witnesses
   Both in speaking and more in practices.

4. Lasting glory. . .

87   FEASTS OF APOSTLES   Matins: third nocturn

1. Thrones of kings and the wise philosophers,
   Placed on high in the seats of councillors,
   These submit to the Lord as servitors.

2. Feeble citizens soften violence;
   Simple answers compete with eloquence;
   Small disorders can gain world prominence.

102

3. Hence with swords do the kings seek victory;
   Thence philosophers practice fluency;
   Yet these miracles work more mightily.

4. Lasting glory. . .

88   FEASTS OF APOSTLES   Lauds

1. Fools to many in this world's quality,
   Christ has chosen to doom philosophy.
   What is proud will be crushed in misery.

2. Nothing polished, and no rhetorical
   Verbal elegance serves as passable.
   Faith's simplicity makes it natural.

3. Now has Cicero lost his eloquence;
   Aristotle gave silence relevance;
   Simple men can explain God's providence.

4. Lasting glory. . .

89 and 90 are hymns for St. Peter and St. Paul, labeled simply prior and alter, though # 90 is about Peter alone and # 91 is for Paul. The first stanza of # 89 may well reflect the Investiture Controversy, discussed in the Introduction. Stanza 1 of # 90 refers to John 21. 15-17, in "Pastor ovium gregis Domini," and to Matthew 16. 19, in "claviger." # 92 reflects the tradition that the eagle can look directly into the sun without harm. # 93 has many levels of symbolism: the four-horse chariot of Christ in the Gospel stories; the wine press from Isaiah 63.3 where the Lord says,

> Torcular calcavi solus. . .calcavi eos in furore meo, et conculcavi eos in ira mea; et aspersus est sanguis eorum super vestimenta mea.

> I have trodden the winepress alone. . . In my anger I trod them down, trampled them in my wrath. Their juice spattered my garments, and all my clothes are stained. (Jerusalem Bible.)

The refreshment of the faithful refers to the Eucharist. # 95 gives the signs of the four evangelists in tradition: St. Matthew as a man, St. Mark as a lion, St. Luke a sacrificial calf, and St. John an eagle. # 96 contains figures from the first chapter of Ezekiel's vision.

89   FEAST OF SS. PETER AND PAUL   Prior

1. Toward the fisherman's door with reverence
   Comes the emperor bent in penitence,
   Praying God in the way of supplicants.

2. Paul no less in the praise he merited
   Wears the diadem, gemmed and garlanded;
   Virgin, white; and as martyr, blood-spotted.

3. Blessed princes of this world's heraldry,
   Friends in war and in death's extremity,
   Now this day have obtained eternity.

4. Lasting glory. . .

1. Chief apostle, the church's ornament,
   Shepherd, tending the flock's good nourishment,
   Watch the sheep with a care as reverent.

2. Yet you practice your skill more usefully;
   Draw your net for mankind with charity;
   Keep the pledge of the Lord's humanity.

3. First key-bearer of heaven's palaces,
   Reach your hand to us, open passages,
   Raise us up whom the Lord acknowledges.

4. Lasting glory. . .

91   FEAST OF ST. PAUL

1. Paul, the trumpet of God in primacy,
   Drawing thunder from heaven steadily,
   Scatter strangers and build one family.

2. You as teacher became preeminent,
   Made the vessel for gentiles' nourishment,
   All those drinking from wisdom's complement.

3. Once this Benjamin joyed in plundering,
   Shared his spoils in the evening's gathering;
   Now feeds doctrine divine and life-giving.[8]

4. This rhinoceros once untamable,
   Tied and bound by the Lord, and peaceable,
   Turns the valleys to make them arable.[9]

5. Now the master can praise his enemy
   Whom he knows to be dealing prudently,
   Filled with zeal for the sons of charity.[10]

6. Lasting glory. . .

----

8. Genesis 49.27.

9. A metaphor from the <u>Moralia</u> of Gregory the Great.

10. This stanza is added by Fr. Chrysogonus from the
    MS.

92   FEAST OF ST. JOHN THE EVANGELIST

1. Heaven's height is the eagle's boundary;
   There his nest has been hidden cunningly,
   Sheltered safe in the Lord's divinity.

2. He who looks on the sun's full radiance,
   Sensing joy in its true beneficence,
   Strengthens sight as he feeds his vigilance.

3. From its fire and heat come substances,
   Warmth of life, and the light of images,
   Clear daylight in the heaven's brightnesses.

4. Lasting glory. . .

93   FEASTS OF EVANGELISTS   Matins: first nocturn
                                   9 syllables, as in the Latin
                                   four-line rhyme.

1. Christ in the Gospellers' harnessing
   Tasted the winepress of suffering.
   Grapes newly pressed from the clustering
   Freshen the hearts of those worshiping.

2. Know that the scripture's New Testament
   Is in the four horses evident.
   We in the church know the heaven-sent
   Word of the Lord as intelligent.

3. Four are the wheels of the vehicle,
   Rolls of the book evangelical,
   Written in prophecies mystical;
   Here we extol them in ritual.

4. Glory to God in the Trinity,
   Spirit and Son in the Unity;
   One in the Godhead and majesty,
   Three in the persons' equality.

93   A simplified meter from the above,
             as an alternate.

1. The four-horse chariot of Christ
   Presents the winepress of the Lord,
   Where clusters in the cup sufficed
   To freshen faithful hearts restored.

2. The chariot we hold to be
    The holy Gospel's four-fold word,
    Where all the churches now agree
    The very voice of God is heard.

3. The wheels that roll the chariot
    Recall the four evangelists,
    To whose narration we allot
    The highest honor that exists.

4. To Father glory as to Son,
    To Spirit as our Paraclete;
    To all as God and Lord in one,
    Though three in persons yet discrete.

94   FEASTS OF EVANGELISTS   Matins: second nocturn
                                  Adjusted meter

1. Think of the cross as the press;
    Wine is produced under stress.
    Christ in his mystic duress
    Suffered to give us redress.

2. Sending the Lord to the tree,
    Symbol of fruitfulness, we
    Bring to the cross mystery:
    What our salvation may be.

3. Prophets who spoke of the Lord
    Could not see him they adored.
    Those who came later reward
    Faith with full vision restored.

4. Glory to Father and Son,
    Paraclete also as one;
    Severance here there is none,
    Unity never undone.

95   FEASTS OF EVANGELISTS   Matins: third nocturn

1. Here what the prophecies designate
    Creatures of heaven are animate.
    Four in appearance are separate;
    Mysteries truly we celebrate.

107

2. He on the right is humanity,
   With him a lion in company;
   Place for a calf is made equally;
   High up the eagle flies mightily.

3. Four-fold in wings they are vigilant,
   Each in its countenance different.
   All-seeing eyes are beneficent;
   Even behind they are prescient.

4. Glory to God in the Trinity,
   Spirit and Son in the Unity;
   One in the Godhead and majesty,
   Three in the persons' equality.

96   FEASTS OF EVANGELISTS   Lauds

1. Going and coming unceasingly,
   Standing in order consistently,
   Riding the wheels with resiliency,
   Here is the Spirit's vitality.

2. Straight are their feet in their traversing,
   Cleft like a calf with an opening;
   Made as from copper and glistening,
   Forward, they seem to be hastening.

3. Holding a lamp like a meteor,
   Brighter than embers and gaudier,
   They while they seem to be steadier
   Run and return as a courier.

4. Glory to God. . .

97-100 show Abelard's ingenuity in combining meters to form a stanza, changing the length of the line within the stanza. The military theme is prominent with the mention of David's citadel from 2 Samuel 5.7 in # 100. The word virtus is used with a double meaning, of the physical strength of the army and of the moral strength of a Christian. The use of cognates in the first stanza of # 97 is characteristic: certaminum and certantium; inermes and armatos.

97   FEASTS OF MARTYRS   Matins: first nocturn
                Four-line rhyme, internal
                rhyme in the last four lines.

1.   God is sun and shield of all,
            Crown for martyrs at their fall;
            He it is who caused the brawl;
            He the palm at martyr's call.
            You avail through helpless man,
            You subdue the partisan.
            When the inner life began,
            Love was fighting in the van.
             Strength and virtue trust this armor,
             Show a naked breast to clamor.
            They on right hand as on left hand fortify;
            As a buckler, every danger they defy.
            In the battle, they though feeble never fly.
            Hope unbidden, faith unshaken they apply.

2.   Through this faith the martyr's breast
            Seemed a tower to attest
            Strength for all mankind oppressed,
            Standing motionless, at rest.
            War machines are brought to bear,
            Great in number, here and there;
            Stones in masses through the air
            Batter virtue everywhere.
             All the outward world is fighting;
             God alone brings inner healing.
            Sword and fire, hostile ire, ravage us,
            Knowing hardly whether man be virtuous.
            Blows come thickly, raining quickly, venomous,
            But from heaven help is given, saving us.

3. Harsh they are, great they are, combats with
                                        righteousness;
    Simple and few they are, matched with the
                                        blessedness.
    Father, whose gifts they are, yours is the
                                        holiness.

98   FEASTS OF MARTYRS   Matins: second nocturn

1.   All of torture's instruments
        Use on these their violence;
        So the martyr's innocence
        May display its influence.
        Fire purifies the gold.
        Shapes it in its proper mold;
        Mustard only takes its hold
        When its germ is crushed and rolled.
        Tools of iron have their function;
        All things work their own destruction.
    Stones are pounded and when rounded wear away.
    Trees may sicken as they quicken in decay.
    Men are joyful, some are mournful equally,
    In affliction of the Christian soldiery.

2.   Prison, chains, and infamy,
        Whips, exposure shamefully,
        Nakedness, with hunger's plea,
        Warnings of the penalty,
        Fire, drowning, death by sword,
        Horses' hoofs, the wooden board,
        Every kind of gallows-cord,
        Bought with every strength outpoured;
        But, that death may be extended,
        Death is held lest pain be ended.
    Thus the martyrs under tortures long to die,
    What the soldier, though he murder, will deny.
    Here are maidens' tender persons mixed with men,
    As in hardship, so in friendship even then.

3.   Harsh they are. . .

1.
       Princes of the demons fight
       With this world as satellite;
       Men of Christ in heaven's might
       Conquer with their moral right.
       Nor can so great victory,
       Neither this militia, be
       Lacking women's dignity,
       Matching glory easily.
     As the strong man, so the tender
     Woman fights and triumphs further.
   Thus they rank in heaven's royal battle line,
   Amazons whose place with heroes we assign.
   Though with mortal body weak and senses fine,
   They prevail with grace less human than divine.

2.
       Men and women, man and wife,
       Brothers, sisters, in this strife,
       Sons with those who gave them life,
       Stand where warfare is most rife.
       Woman stirs the heart of man,
       Strengthens sons as guardian;
       She preserves for heaven's plan
       Those whose life on earth began,
     Following them straight to heaven,
     Made for Christ, a whole oblation.
   Sister urges brother on as they contend;
   Words and actions show the spirit they defend.
   What could young men do but battle for the Lord
   When they see the warring maidens' strength
                                       outpoured?

3.   Harsh they are. . .

1.   David's tower gives to these
       Surety from their enemies.
       God is strength to weakened knees,
       Shield and walls that none can seize,
       Arms for all the martyr throng;
       Strength from heaven makes them strong,
       Ample force to skirmish long,
       Warring with whatever wrong.
       Disciplined in Christ they struggle,
       Fight, and learn to mock the devil.
Sturdier than hardest iron, sealed and tried,
Axe and hammer on their armor turn aside.
Here the soldier hedged around by hostile pride
Taunts detractors for their efforts falling
                                        wide.

2.   In this tower, Lord, we pray,
       May we lodge as well as they.
       Walling up in every way
       Wall and dyke and siege array.
       Let no entry be allowed
       To the hostile, savage crowd.
       Men whose prayer herein is vowed,
       Let us be with sleep endowed.
       And by how much we are lacking,
       Shelter us with stronger backing.
If we fail to bear the cross of chivalry,
Let us simply stand to aid the infantry;
If we cannot earn the palm of victory,
Grant us to avoid a mean disloyalty.

3.   Harsh they are. . .

The feast of the Holy Innocents is kept on
December 28 in order to place near the nativity of
Christ the death of the innocent children slain by
Herod, in his search for the child whom the Magi
pointed to as a threat to his kingdom, told in Matthew
2, 1-18. Abelard describes the drama in these hymns, #
101-104, and in # 102, 5-6, he uses a story from
Macrobius' Saturnalia:

> When Augustus heard that among the children
> under two whom Herod, king of the Jews, had
> ordered killed in Syria, his own son also
> died, he said, "It is better to be Herod's
> pig than to be his son."

Rachel weeping for her children is a scene taken
from Jeremiah 31.15.[1]

101   THE HOLY INNOCENTS   Matins: first nocturn

1. At the coming
   Of the real king
     Does the tyrant
   Fear destruction
   Of his portion
     By the infant.

2. When the Wise Men
   Tell of proven
     Stellar portents,
   Much they trouble
   King and people
     With their presents.

3. So the wicked
   King, incited
     Toward the infant,
   Dared empower
   Infant slaughter,
   Unrepentant.

----

1. Macrobius' story is found in Venatus, Joannes
   Rivisu, Liber Secundus, Primi Diei Saturnaliorum
   (1513) ch. X. "Quum audisset inter pueros quos in
   Syria Herodes rex Iudaeorum intra bimatum iussit
   interfici, filium quoque eius occisum, ait, 'Melius
   est Herodis porcum esse quam filium.'"

4. Christ was hunted,
   Persecuted,
     In the children;
   Christ the trophy
   For the worthy
     Crowned in heaven.

102   THE HOLY INNOCENTS   Matins: second nocturn

1. Despot ruler
   And oppressor,
     All surpassing,
   Yet more cruel
   And uncivil
     Brutalizing;

2. Towards the infants
   As opponents
     He is moving,
   And on no one
   But his nation
     Is he turning.

3. Wrath and anger,
   Fury never
     Comparable,
   Lost him children
   The old Roman
     Wolf would fondle.

4. But the urgent
   New commandment
     Did not order
   His own infant
   By his agent
     Kept from slaughter.

5. When Augustus
   Heard this justice,
     It amused him;
   And his goodness
   At this harshness
     Mocked the victim.

6. "He is now dead
   Who by Herod
     Was begotten.
   Pigs are better
   Cared for rather
     Than his children."

114

THE HOLY INNOCENTS   Matins: third nocturn

1. To the suckling
   Mother running
     As to battle,
   Toward the children,
   Struck and fallen,
     Run the people.

2. While the baby
   Likes the shiny
     Swords advancing,
   Soon to perish
   In the onrush,
     He is laughing.

3. When was spoken
   Seen or written,
     Such abasement?
   From our nature,
   From man's honor,
     What so distant?

4. Why on naked
   Christ, O Herod,
     Look so fearsome?
   "This world," said he,
   "Is not ready
     For my kingdom."

5. Of the lasting
   Things, not falling,
     He is ruler.
   He has taken
   Nothing human
     Who gives better.

1. Rama listens,
   Hears and questions
      Rachel weeping;
   For her children,
   Struck and fallen,
      Still lamenting.

2. Torn as martyrs
   Lie the members
      Of the infants,
   Where their bleeding,
   Milk outspreading,
      Wets the pavements.

3. Head and heart bent
   In bereavement,
      Mourning on them,
   She embraces
   Human pieces
      In her bosom.

4. Blinded frenzy
   Drives her madly,
      Tears her bosom.
   She as woman
   Is of human
      Love the victim.

5. Though they perished,
   They have furnished
      Life for others.
   Nothing purchased,
   Still the richest
      Are their treasures.

6. Treasure heightened,
   Life was shortened.
      They too even
   In their dying,
   Not in speaking,
      Made profession.

105-106, the two hymns for St. Denis, were doubtless written before Abelard's discovery from Bede that the abbey's patron was the bishop of Corinth rather than of Athens. St. Denis is called Cephalophorus from the story that he carried his head in his hands after it was severed from his body by the pagan Gauls. # 107 is the story of St. Aigulph who was abbot at Lérins in the seventh century and gave his name to a priory in Provins where Abelard rested after his flight from St. Denis.[2] St. Aigulph was murdered by his monks because of his severe rule. Why Abelard should write a hymn for St. Eustace is not known, but he tells the complete story of the martyr.

105   ST. DENIS   <u>Prior</u>: Matins

1. To you, our bishop, bishop's praise;
   To you, our martyr, martyr's bays;
   Philosopher in stature grand,
   Apostle to the Gallic land.

2. Through you the people in this Gaul,
   Untamed and insolent to all,
   Were tamed, and found their strength sufficed
   To come beneath the yoke of Christ.

3. You only, you most wondrously,
   Have turned them from idolatry;
   You loosed them from the devil's ward,
   And made them over to the Lord.

4. Pray, Father Denis, for us all,
   We faithful, when you hear us call,
   And for this kingdom's blessedness,
   Which you by martyrdom possess.

5. The unbegotten Father sing,
   And praise his holy Son the King.
   The Paraclete's own gifts suffice
   Beside that welcome sacrifice.

----

2. DACL, 5,2, 1709.

1. Acknowledged soldier of the Lord,
   Who claimed of God his due reward,
   You made yourself the sacrifice,
   In battle gave the ransom's price.

2. You brought him there your very life,
   A votive offering in the strife,
   To him who was the sacrifice,
   And gave for us the Father's price.

3. Nor did disciples dare by-pass
   The sacrifice of such a Mass,
   With whom you were accustomed most
   To share the consecrated Host.

4. When nature broke its formal bands,
   You held your head within your hands;
   That head struck off by pagan sword,
   Which you would offer to the Lord.

5. The unbegotten Father. . .

107   ST. AIGULPH   Adjusted meter
                      Abelard's irregular rhyme

1. This for Aigulphus, the martyr and priest,
   Marks his red star that arose in the East.
   Star to the stars, from his life here released,
   Now celebrates a perpetual feast.

2. Justly the martyrs are put on the right;
   This they have earned by their blood in the fight;
   Wherefore the palace's royal delight
   Sets them in purple in royalty's sight.

3. Martyrdom doubled the victor's reward,
   Once in monastic life, then by the sword.
   Following close on the footsteps of Christ,
   Killed by his monks, he is worthily priced.

4. But what was left by his sons in their crime,
   Sought by disciples, is kept for all time.
   Witness to this is the land of Champagne,
   Offering gifts for the relics they gain.

108   ST. EUSTACHIUS   Matins
Adjusted meter

1. Heavenly courts praise the soldiers in war;
   Knights who are joined with them come to the fore.
   Best of them all is the martyr whose day
   Gives us the light of Eustochius' ray.

2. Soldier and captain, excelling on earth,
   Shines as a jewel of martyrdom's worth.
   Pagan Cornelius,[3] whose faith and whose zeal
   Merits a place in the Christian ideal.

3. Hunter himself, whom the Hunter surprised,
   Turned to the Lord to accept him baptized.
   Husband and wife with the children begin
   Sharing the life of renewal within.

4. Once the baptism has washed us of stain,
   How great the virtue, so great is the pain;
   Thus for the Lord we make purer the gold;
   So when death comes, it has loosened its hold.

5. Trials will temper a heart made of stone;
   Suffering melts even iron ingrown.
   Who is not moved to compassionate tears,
   Seeing another's disconsolate fears?

6. But because tenderness draws us to weep,
   So will the blessedness fill us as deep.
   Thus will our weeping, our tears, and our sighs
   Bring us through time to the joy of the prize.

7. Praise to the Lord, and eternal renown!
   His is the grace giving martyrs the crown.
   Here through their death they make speed to the
   Lord.
   There after death is their lasting reward.

----

3. Acts 10.

119

1. Satan tried Job with a lighter assault
   Even than saints, be the scribe not at fault.
   Job lost the children in sorrow and strife,
   But for his comfort he still had his wife.

2. Job was allowed to remain among friends,
   Seeking relief that companionship lends.
   This one with children, his goods overthrown,
   Fled with his wife to a country unknown.

3. Forced to bind over his wife while at sea,
   Seizing his children, he hastened to flee.
   Then that the burden lack nothing in weight,
   Satan made sure of the two children's fate.

4. Shortly a wolf made away with his son;
   Under his eyes came a lion for one.
   Family, property, all were destroyed;
   Now in the fields he is wholly employed.

5. Job received double in goods from the Lord,
   Happiness, length of days, fully restored;
   This one recovered his children and wife,
   Witnesses when he should give up his life.

6. How is this family dear to the Lord!
   How undiminished its righteous accord!
   Where with his wife and his children he went,
   Faith and his suffering made the ascent.

7. Praise to the Lord. . .

    # 110-113 are hymns for the feasts of confessors,
those who confessing Christ proclaimed themselves
Christians. As with all his hymns for saints, Abelard
emphasizes that the credit for their good deeds and
strength belongs to God and not to humans. The meters
again are complicated.

110   FEASTS OF CONFESSORS   Matins: first nocturn

1. Worthy praise of godly men offered heartily,
    Psalms and hymns and holy songs with sincerity,
    Now the church awards her sons forever sure,
    Trusting them in turn for prayer intense and
                                            pure.
    King and Father, here we pay you thanks and honor to
                                            the Son,
    For the gifts from heaven sent us, gifts of grace the
                                            Victim won.
            Yours they are, whoso are justified;
            Yours they are, those who are sanctified.

2. All good deeds of these are gifts only in your
                                            grace,
    All our praise and hymns of these, glory from your
                                            face.
    He who praises sings for you his loving heart,
    You in them and they in you in equal part.
    All their festivals are lighted only by your charity;
    All your benefits recited for them in our litany.
            Yours they are, whoso are justified;
            Yours they are, those who are sanctified.

3. Glory to the God of saints, wonderful in these,
    Who is all in all to them, whom they love to
                                            please.
    This their God of living power as he wills,
    Highest prudence, righteousness in those he fills;
    Him we know as willing good, accomplished by his
                                            active thought;
    His supreme and holy goodness leaves no doubt in what
                                            he wrought.
            Yours they are, whoso are justified;
            Yours they are, those who are sanctified.

1. You alone give abstinence, holding in the flesh;
    You alone give continence, ruling it afresh.
    You alone whose gift it is can add to these
    Willingness to use it with intent to please.
    To a human you have given grace to work your
                                            prodigies;
    As the mover you inspire hearts with heaven's
                                            imageries.
            Yours they are, whoso are justified;
            Yours they are, those who are sanctified.

2. Those possessed by devils' arts they can liberate;
    Confidently others' hearts they can animate.
    Paralytics by their healing they restore,
    And the leper's flesh by praying cleanse once
                                            more.
    Eyes to open, steps to strengthen, power to the dead
                                            to rise,
    What is needed is provided; you complete the
                                            enterprise.
            Yours they are, whoso are justified;
            Yours they are, those who are sanctified.

3. Glory to the God of saints. . .

112   FEASTS OF CONFESSORS   Matins: third nocturn

1. Life on earth for these became Friday's sacrifice,
    Where with Christ in abstinence they have paid the
                                            price.
    As he told them, they must too take up the cross,
    Just as Paul in crucifixion purged his dross.
    After this the peace of mind is as the sabbath of
                                            the soul;
    On the eighth day you will give them back their
                                            bodies' clothing whole.
            Yours they are, whoso are justified;
            Yours they are, those who are sanctified.

2. Persecution's bloody sword did not bring them down,
   But a will and mind prepared won them still the
                                              crown.
   Though the body did not bear the iron point,
   Still confessors bring their purpose to anoint.
   Though the jailor, though the torment cease their
                                    work of every kind,
   You who look within the heart can but reward a
                                         martyr's mind.
        Yours they are, whoso are justified;
        Yours they are, those who are sanctified.

3. Glory to the God of saints. . .

113   FEASTS OF CONFESSORS   Lauds

1. Final rites of worthy men call us to their praise;
   Funerals of wicked men call back evil days.
   Death but draws the good man to eternity;
   Death redoubled grinds the wicked hopelessly.
   Life was heavy for the holy; chains and prison here
                                           they knew;
   Unencumbered, no more hindered, now his soul has fled
                                              to you.
        Yours they are, whoso are justified;
        Yours they are, those who are sanctified.

2. When the blessed soul at last comes to you in
                                              peace.
   Who can hope to know the joy and its long increase?
   How much dignity is there before his eye!
   Who can count the throng whom you can satisfy?
   No unworthy soul can fully see the glory of your
                                              face,
   Where you joy in those in heaven, bringing us to
                                       your embrace.
        Yours they are, whoso are justified;
        Yours they are, those who are sanctified.

3. Glory to the God of saints. . .

   # 114-117 are for St. John Baptist, always
prominent in Christian art and next to St. Mary after
the Lord. In John 1. 23, he is called the forerunner
of the Lord, quoting Isaiah 40,3, a voice crying in the
wilderness; vox clamantis in deserto.

114 FEAST OF ST. JOHN BAPTIST Matins: first
nocturn

1. Birthday this of holy John,
   Harbinger of Christ his Lord,
   He who stirs the heart of man
   To the joys of heaven's board.

2. Great this man, his message great,
   Say the Gospels; none his peer.
   They beyond the ancient line
   Rank the last prophetic seer.

3. Others bear but thirty-fold,
   Sixty-fold the fruit of some.
   Hundred-fold the wealth of John,
   Herald of the Word to come.

4. Glory to the Father, God,
   Equal be it to the Son;
   To the Spirit as to them
   Our co-equal orison.

115 FEAST OF ST. JOHN BAPTIST Matins: second
nocturn

1. None but the archangel told,
   Sent from God, this prophet's birth,
   He the same who soon would call
   God the Son from heaven to earth.

2. Unbelieving, hearing not,
   Fell the father's rebel voice,
   Till the son, himself as mute,
   Witnessed to the father's choice.

3. John enclosed within the womb
   Knew the very Godhead here.
   What his voice could not pronounce
   Joy would prophesy as near.

4. Glory to. . .

116 FEAST OF ST. JOHN BAPTIST Matins: third
nocturn

1. One the aged man begot,
   This one was by virgin born.
   Grace in turn on each prevailed,
   Nature's hold a moment torn.

2. Tender age sought out a test
   In the desert's discipline.
   Harsh the silent life alone,
   Leading others out of sin.

3. Here so marvelous a war
   As of word as well as deed,
   Watchers hopeful of the Christ
   Saw fulfilment of man's need.

4. This the prophet's prophet now,
   He whom very Christ approved,
   Showing none could be as great
   As the man the Spirit moved.

5. Glory to. . .

117   FEAST OF ST. JOHN BAPTIST   Lauds

1. To prepare Messiah's way
   John the herald came before.
   He alone could meet the Lord
   To baptize him on the shore.

2. His the witness by his word,
   Through which truth has fought its way.
   His the lonely herald cry,
   Waking truth's illumined ray.

3. Virgin saint and martyr both,
   John has earned the diadem.
   He who hailed the Lord as lamb
   Searched his steps and pressed on them.

4. Glory to . . .

    # 118 is for St. Benedict, the only hymn in
sapphic meter, and without rhyme. The use of cognates
is in Abelard's style. In stanza 3 we find memorandus
and memoras; in stanza 5, qualia and quanta and quibus;
there is repetition of terra from 5 to 6; and benedicta
and Benedictum.

1. Offering praises come we, Christ, to honor
    Benedict, holy man of your own pleasing,
    Whose is the shining life reflecting heaven,
        Light of your dayspring.

2. Benedict humbly praying to you for us,
    Asks as a client, begging favor for us,
    He to whose praises we address our hymning,
        Singing this strophe.

3. Mindful of conquest of the adversary,
    Mindful he makes us of his own deserving.
    May you be mindful of us through his praying,
        Christ ever loving.

4. Called as by promise Benedict from childhood,
    Later he added meaning from your blessing,
    Joy of your grace and merit of his virtue,
        Victory's warrant.

5. What was his own life, this the man we honor,
    How great his healing, all his working tells us;
    Earth with his doctrine fills her every corner,
        So we all know him.

6. Earth with her sorrow in our sins committed,
    Offering only thorns and trouble to us,
    Now can return us benediction richly,
        Benedict's trophy.

7. Wherefore he labored, wonderfully skilful,
    Working a certain spiritual harrow;
    Rule of his living, mirror of true doctrine,
        Christian and holy.

8. Glory to Father, over all the highest,
    So to the Father's Word above all other.
    Glory from all men, praising you, the Spirit,
        Give we in honor.

119 is for St. Gildas, the Breton saint for whom the abbey was named where Abelard was abbot.

119   ST. GILDAS   Adjusted meter

1. Given as light for the lamps here below,
   Gildas' whole life and experience glow,
   Teaching with words and inciting with deeds,
   Finding the lost, urging those whom he leads.

2. Lanterns reflect from the Lord of the light,
   Not to be hidden but set on a height,
   Star for the castaways, placed by the Sun,
   Whereby the roads to our fatherland run.

3. This light is constant, the star of the West,
   Reaching all earth in its resolute quest,
   Even to Brittany's desolate land,
   Where the vast waves of the ocean expand.

4. Here there had lived a belligerent race,
   Who when the battle had threatened disgrace,
   Shouting the war cry of Gildas' appeal,
   Followed his lead through the enemy's steel.

5. Thus has the country made use of his prayer;
   Even in battle they trust in his care.
   Glory be theirs and to all in this place,
   Given the favor of heavenly grace.

120-127 are about saints who were women, for whom Abelard had high praise. In his letter to Astrolabe, his son, he says that they are preeminent in merits for the very reason that their sex is fragile:

Quanto plus fragilis mulieribus sexus habetur,
Tanto eius virtus praeminet in meritis.[1]

Mary of Egypt was a fifth century recluse who in her early life was a prostitute in Egypt but joined a pilgrimage to Jerusalem where she repented and went into solitude beyond the Jordan and there lived for forty-seven years as an ascetic. In # 125 Abelard brings in women who were heroines in Israel: Deborah, Judith, and Jephthah's daughter, who risked their lives for the nation.[2] In # 127 he names Anna and Elizabeth, New Testament matrons from St. Luke's Gospel.

120   COMMON OF VIRGINS   Matins: first nocturn

1. Christ is bridegroom; maid and martyr is the bride
   Whose oblation sees her day thus sanctified.
   Two oblations cultivate the present feast:
   Maid her body; martyr overcame the beast.
       In her honor let the psalms resound,
       Let the readings then in place be found.

2. Two oblations meet but rarely in a man.
   Fruitful woman bears more sorrow than he can.
   More the wonder, since her strength has shorter
                                          span;
   Maiden virtue in the martyr far outran.
       Sacrifices thus are welcome more
       By how much her honor sets its store.

3. Still unspotted, sound in body as in soul,
   Truth she offers since her virgin heart is whole.
   At the altar praise him whom her gifts extoll;
   Offer symbols, crimson blood and heifer's foal.
       There the shadow, here the truth appears,
       If the symbol still in truth adheres.

----

1. PL 178, 1764C. As the sex in women is held more fragile, So their valor excels the more in merit.

2. Judges 4-5; the book of Judith; Judges 11, 29-39.

4. She who wholly consecrates to God her will
   Gives her body willingly to man to kill;
   Once her spirit consecrated to the Lord,
   Now her body offers to the hostile sword.
     His the beauty, his the majesty
     Who created so amazingly.

121   COMMON OF VIRGINS   Matins: second nocturn

1. Though in all the saints the virtue comes from God,
   Yet the path shines brightest where the martyrs trod.
   Since to women too he gives the victory,
   Who would not exalt their grace deservedly?
     For as in their sex their strength is less,
     So much more there is in it to bless.

2. Tortures cruelly devised of every kind
   Cannot overcome her steadfast strength of mind.
   Either woman's valor comes direct from God
   Or she finds it easy to support the rod.
     Still we know for each the better road
     Means the one that God who called them showed.

3. Love is strong as death for those who know the Lord.
   Fire itself has not the power love has stored.
   Many waters cannot quench the ardent flame,
   Love unconquerable making good its claim.
     Nor is ever either sex too weak
     Once it learns to hear love's courage speak.

4. Why admire bearded youths alone for this?
   Maidens soft and fragile win the martyr's bliss.
   Let the stronger man with grace accept the shame,
   When the weaker earns with equal right this fame.
     His the beauty, his the majesty
     Who created so amazingly.

122   COMMON OF VIRGINS   Matins: third nocturn

1. How the bride is constant in her faith to Christ
   All her life has witnessed, though her death sufficed
   Guarding well her body whole and undefiled,
   This she offered freely, fully reconciled.
     Virgin bride and virgin bridegroom both,
     Martyrs with their first espousals' oath.

2. Such a bridegroom rightly merits such a bride.
   She will follow in the way his footsteps guide.
   Like in beauty of their consecrated flesh,
   So in death this love unites the two afresh.
    Other maidens walk behind the spouse,
    But for her more favor he allows.

3. Heaven's queen is held upon the bridegroom's right;
   Others follow in a throng in virgin white.
   She, resplendent in her robe of cloth of gold,
   Leads on those whose crown it is her right to hold.
    Surely this is gold of quality,
    Uncorrupted, shining splendidly.

4. Garlands woven with the lily and the rose
   Mark the virtue that the virgin martyr shows.
   Odors brought to Christ are sweetly redolent;
   Martyrs bring the rose, and virgins lily's scent.
    Even clothes denote their holy place;
    Royal scarlet, whiteness of their grace.

5. Beautiful processions, sandals on their feet,
   Hear the bridegroom's praise in songs their hearts
                                          repeat.
   What their course and order is has been designed;
   Where their movement carries them must be defined.
    His the beauty, his the majesty
    Who created so amazingly.

123   COMMON OF VIRGINS   Lauds

1. Rising as the morning light, she walks on high,
   Bound to him, her heavenly spouse, in marriage tie.
   Here on earth, betrothed to him, she made her vow;
   There she lives, his wife, and in his presence now.
    Here by faith betrothal rites allured;
    There eternal marriage joys assured.

2. Angels has he for attendance in his train,
   Angel guardians within his own domain.
   Singing of the joys of heaven's marriage bed,
   Angels in procession point where she is led.
    Here the virgin meets the virgins' band;
    There the martyr sees where martyrs stand.

130

3. When she comes to meet her spouse escorted so,
   Quiet in the strong embrace his arms bestow,
   Who can say what glory she enjoys at last?
   What conception have we of a joy so vast?
     Mortal mind can nothing here discern
     Till the spirit feels and love can learn.

4. There are joys which human eye has never seen,
   Nor can mortal hearts perceive a sense so keen.
   What with those who love him he has always shared,
   This he has through time eternally prepared.
     His the beauty, his the majesty,
     Who created so amazingly.

124   FEASTS OF HOLY WOMEN   Matins: first nocturn

1. We who take our wound of sin from either sex,
   We receive from either too the good effects.
   God has put on manhood from a maiden's word
   Whereby woman's plea as well as man's is heard.
     Saving grace has sprung from woman kind;
     Whence the fault, there comes the grace we find.

2. Since her sex is lower in its nature's rank,
   So the farther in its sin and guilt it sank.
   Wonderfully then divine forbearance came,
   Raising by a larger grace her high acclaim.
     So consider how in gentle pace
     From his virgin mother comes her place.

3. Who can number all the holy virgin choir,
   Pressing on her to delight in and admire?
   After these, who does not know the widows' lot,
   Numberless, whose vows no witness has forgot?
     For in holy marriage nothing fails
     Where desire of heaven still prevails.

4. After all of these, regard the prostitute;
   Magdalen and she of Egypt bore their fruit.
   Where the blame at first was plainly evident,
   Virtue's holy flowers were luxuriant.
     His the beauty, his the majesty
     Who created so amazingly.

1. Giving honor to virginity's reward
    As to make a virgin mother of the Lord,
    How in worth and value can we then endow
    Other states of women as their gifts allow?
     How the many holy states agree,
     Sacred scripture gives us history.

2. Paradise's first inhabitant was man;
    He outside and Eve within when life began.
    Thus the place itself gives her the primacy,
    Marking her creation blest especially.
     What is built from Adam's rib and side
     Has the strength his bone and flesh provide.

3. Women's strength in many things has greater force
    When the bravery of man has run its course.
    Deborah as judge held fast in Israel;
    Holofernes by a widow's courage fell.
     Seven sons who with their mother died
     Earned for her the church's honest pride.

4. Jephthah's daughter, when he conquered in the fight
    Gave her life into her father's hand to smite,
    Choosing for herself the promised sacrifice,
    Lest her father's vow become a false device.
     His the beauty, his the majesty
     Who created so amazingly.

126   FEASTS OF HOLY WOMEN   Matins: third nocturn

1. If it be allowed for women to contend
    In the steadiness of virtues they defend,
    Who indeed of heroes in his strength of mind
    Equals Jephthah's daughter in her fate assigned?
     Lest her father's vow be falsified,
     For her father willingly she died.

2. How she would have born a martyr's agony,
    Forced to turn against the Lord in perjury,
    Now appears in constancy of virgin life,
    Spiritual grace that arms her for the strife.
     So the solemn hymns for virgins' days
     Celebrate the virgin's death with praise.

3. Countless men with deeds of courage and renown
    Freed their brethren from the foe and won the crown.
    Esther by herself has set her people free,
    Thereby earned a celebration by decree,
       So that clearly women's strength could show
       How where needed it can freely flow.

4. By how much the weakness of the sex is known,
    By so much the wonder of its strength is shown.
    So much more of praise its excellence commands,
    Raising high the claim to heaven's own demands.
       His the beauty, his the majesty
       Who created so amazingly.

127   FEASTS OF HOLY WOMEN   Lauds

1. Let us come to saints of our own time at last,
    When the grace of heaven flows as in time past.
    Who will not perceive from every sort of gauge
    Women to excel in grace in this our age?
       After Mary, think of Anna's name,
       Then Elizabeth deserves the same.

2. She who held the foot of Christ devotedly
    Made him truly Christ, "anointed," bodily.[3]
    Mysteries of priest and king are here arrayed,
    By a woman's understanding love displayed.
       Woman is in birth the instrument;
       So a woman shows the sacrament.

3. She who poured the spices for his burial
    First beheld him risen on the festival.
    Sinner first, and in her guilt and sins entwined,
    Now in special grace excels all womankind.
       Therefore from a life that sins destroy,
       See conversion's great and holy joy.

----

3. The word Christ in Greek means anointed.

Among women whom Abelard praised is Mary Magdalen, whose story is in Luke 7, 36-50. Dr. Szövérffy suggests in a footnote that Abelard may have felt special sympathy for Mary Magdalen in that the institutional church was severe with him also.[4] There are other reasons, however, for her inclusion in his calendar, for the church at Vézelay was dedicated to her and had come into notice for its recent reform by the Cluny abbey. It had been founded by Gerard de Rousillon with a title anterior to Cluny, but its discipline had become so relaxed that in 1027 the Cluny abbot took charge and reformed it, even though it had been free from oversight and responsible only to Rome. There was also friction between the town under Count Guillaume de Nevers and the monks of the abbey.[5] Her human story appealed to many.

> It was Mary Magdalen who brought the pilgrims to Vézelay. The abbey claimed to have her entire skeleton, and that was a powerful attraction. . .She herself had been a sinner, it was believed even a prostitute, and yet she was a special friend of Jesus. She would understand, she could explain.[6]

128   ST. MARY MAGDALEN

1. Of the sinner this is the solemnity.
    Sinners with her share the pardon joyfully.
    No one henceforth may despair of sin unshriven,
    For the sins long past are now by love forgiven,
    Only if with sorrow's suffering
    Follows from the heart an offering.

2. Hearts repentant, spirits disciplined in grief;
    No burnt offerings compare to bring relief.
    In the heart man slays the wickedness within;
    Animals so slain can never heal man's sin.
    There each one must sacrifice his will;
    Here another's life leaves penance still.

----

4. HP, vol. II., p. 266, n.

5. Huygens, ed., "Monumenta Vizeliacensis," CC 42, intro.

6. Bamber Gascoigne, The Christians (London 1977), p. 94.

3. There the truth of penitence is in the soul;
    Here similitude of grace, but not the whole.
    There the body; here the body's shadowing.
    There it rests; but this like shadows vanishing.
     Wherefore the beloved sinner's face
     Offered very truth in symbols' place.

4. Rich is every sacrifice of sorrow's tears;
    Weeping is a medicine of wasted years.
    Long may be the time of failure in the past;
    Quick indeed the Lord's forgiveness at the last.
     His the honor, his the majesty,
     But above all, his the charity.

129   ST. MARY MAGDALEN

1. Sharp correction of the church's discipline,
    Lengthy practices of penitence for sin,
    These consume the flesh in watching and in fast;
    These devour the sinner for the sins long past.
     Shame confounds in humbled misery
     Him the church rejected ruthlessly.

2. Nothing done in such disorder comes from God.
    Man knows him as kinder than the judge's rod.
    King and Justice both, he mitigates the laws,
    Nor will he who justly judges every cause
     Wait so long a time of law's delay,
     As the size of penalties men pay.

3. What he knows not will the Pharisee reject,
    Holding pity from the Lord in ill respect,
    While within himself reviling murmurs rise,
    Jesus, judge of hearts, discerns the murmur's guise.
     So he speaks his reason's urgency,
     Why she has deserved his clemency.

4. Mary bound for years in chains of sinfulness
    Now as if released from seven demons' stress,
    Shows her faith become as firm as love was strong.
    So the Lord has taught us how to bless the wrong.
     His the honor, his the majesty,
     But above all, his the charity.

130-133 are hymns for all the saints, again in an unusual meter. In # 133 Abelard mentions the pantheon, from which the pagan gods had been banished by Pope Boniface IV some time between 604 and 610 A.D. Famine and pestilence had so plagued Rome that the Emperor Phocas gave the building to the Christians, who dedicated it to the new <u>Magna Mater</u> instead of Cybele, put a cross on the doors, and sang the <u>Gloria in excelsis</u>; then brought the bones of the Christians from the catacombs to rest there.[7]

130 FESTIVALS OF ALL THE SAINTS   Matins: first
                                                    nocturn

1. Festivals we set to meet   All the saints;
    With solemnities we greet   Human saints.
    Ages joyfully repeat   Faithful saints.

2. When we fail in what we pay   Separately
    Through the year without a day   Carelessly,
    These at last in praise we pay   Solemnly.

3. Praise of saints but comes to you, God alone,
    As the head to whom is due   What we own.
    They so turn their earthly view   Toward the
                                              throne.

4. Yours, O Father, is the power   Totally;
    Yours, O Wisdom, is the hour   Finally;
    Yours, O Spirit, grace to flower Gloriously.

131 FESTIVALS OF ALL THE SAINTS   Matins: second
                                                    nocturn

1. Gate of heaven; of the sky   Open door,
    Matrons, maids to glorify,   Praises pour.
    Supplication multiply   Evermore.

2. Soldiers of the heavenly king's   Battle line
    Fight to crush demonic things,   Yet malign,
    So the rest to man it brings   Be benign.

----

7. Ferdinand Gregorovius, <u>History of the City of Rome</u> (London 1894), vol. II, ch. 4, pp. 105-113.

3. These for our protection here   You have sent.
    Keep us always in your fear,   Their intent.
    We to that same way adhere   As they went.

4. Yours, O Father. . .

132 FESTIVALS OF ALL THE SAINTS   Matins: third
                                                nocturn

1. This the celebration of   All the saints
    Brings the happy notice of   Ancient saints,
    For collected birthdays of   Martyr saints.

2. Here a bridge from Old and New   Testament;
    Prophet's fame and martyr's too   With him went,
    Praising Christ, the Baptist who   Here was sent.

3. Then the grateful church recalls   Generals;
    Then, O Lord, within your walls,   Seneschals;
    Then she finally installs   Corporals.

4. Here the virgins' chorus stands,   Royal line;
    Here among the roses' bands   Lilies twine.
    Purple flowers make the lands   A design.

5. Three ways are the flowers bred   Growing tall.
    You, O Lord, sweet odor spread   To enthrall;
    Flourishing as flowers' head   Over all.

6. Yours, O Father. . .

133   FESTIVALS OF ALL THE SAINTS   Lauds

1. Demon altars now are all   Overturned;
    Idols of the pagans fall,   Justly burned;
    Praise to saints' memorial   Is returned.

2. Here again the faithful meet   Year by year,
    Whom the priests and bishops greet Coming here,
    Laying praises at their feet,   Love sincere.

3. What at one time from the head   Was begun
    In the members in his stead   Now is done.
    Honor by them merited   Has been won.

4. Let the saints whose joy we share   As we praise
    Praise the Lord beyond compare   In amaze,
    Aiding us in constant prayer   On our ways.

137

5. Heaven's soldiery are these   Of the court.
   On your prayers, O Lord, we seize,   Our resort.
   In your name their litanies   Give support.

6. Yours, O Father. . .

The list of hymns for the church year is obviously incomplete, leading us to believe that there are other hymns written by Abelard unkown to us. Dr. Szöverffy ends his introduction in the <u>Hymnarius Paraclitensis I</u> by saying, "The hope exists that, one day, further hymns may be identified as hymns by Abelard, hitherto unrecognized."

BIBLIOGRAPHY

Abelard, Peter, <u>Historia calamitatum</u> PL 178,114-182

Adams, Henry, <u>Mont St. Michel and Chartres</u>
        <u>(N.Y. 1904)</u> chapter 14

Baldwin, Marshall W., <u>The Medieval Church</u>
        <u>(Cornell 1953)</u>

Bark, W.C., <u>Origins of the Medieval World</u>
        <u>(Stanford 1958)</u>

Barraclough, Geoffrey, <u>The Medieval Papacy</u>
        <u>(N.Y. 1968)</u>

Beare, W., <u>Latin Verse and European Song</u>
        <u>(London 1957)</u>

Bennett, J.A.W., <u>Poetry of the Passion</u> (Oxford 1982)

Benton, John, Two unpublished monographs on the
        <u>Historia calamitatum</u>

Bloch, Marc, <u>Feudal Society</u> tr. L.A. Manyon
        <u>(Chicago 1961)</u>

Bouyer, Louis, <u>The Cistercian Heritage</u> tr. E. Liv-
        ingstone (London 1958)

Brooke, Christopher, <u>Medieval Church and Society</u>
        <u>(N.Y. 1972)</u>

Bynum, C.W., "Did the Twelfth Century Discover the
        Individual?" in <u>Journal of Ecclesi-</u>
        <u>astical History</u>, Jan. 1980 (Cambridge
        1980), vol. 31, pp. 1-4

Cabrol, F., <u>St. Benedict</u> (Image 1958)

Chapman, J., <u>Saint Benedict and the Sixth Century</u>
        <u>(Westport, Ct. 1972)</u>

Carré, Meyrick, <u>Realists and Nominalists</u> (Oxford 1946)

Charrier, Charlotte, Héloïse dans l'histoire et dans la légende (Paris 1933)

Chodorow, Stanley, Christian Political Theory and Church Politics in the Mid-Twelfth Century (U. Cal. 1972)

Christ, Ronald, "An Interview with Helen Lang," in Translation Review (Syracuse, N.Y. 1980), vol 5.

Constable, Giles, The Letters of Peter the Venerable (Harvard 1967), vol. 1

Cosby, Ruth, "Oral Delivery in the Middle Ages," in Speculum III, 1936

Daly, Lowrie J., Benedictine Monasticism (N.Y. 1964)

Dawson, Christopher, Medieval Essays (London 1953)

Deanesley, Margaret, A History of the Medieval Church (London 1925)

Delhaye, Philippe, Medieval Christian Philosophy tr. S.J. Tester (N.Y. 1960)

Dronke, Peter, "The 'Hymnarius Paraclitensis' of Joseph Szövérffy" in Mittellateinisches Jahrbuch, vol. 13, 1977, pp. 307-311

Duckett, E.S., Anglo-Saxon Saints and Scholars (N.Y. 1947)

——— The Gateway to the Middle Ages (N.Y. 1938)

Evans, Gillian R., Anselm and Talking About God (Oxford 1978)

Evans, Joan, Monastic Life at Cluny (Archon Books 1958)

Fremantle, Anne, The Age of Belief (Boston 1955)

Fry, Timothy, ed., The Rule of St. Benedict: RB 1980 (Collegeville, Minn. 1981)

Gascoigne, Bamber, The Christians (London 1977)

Gies, Joseph and Frances, Life in a Medieval City
(N.Y. 1973)
——————— Women in the Middle Ages
(N.Y. 1978)

Gilson, Etienne, Heloise and Abelard (Chicago 1951)

Gougaud, Louis, Christianity in Celtic Lands
(London 1932)

Grane, Leif, Peter Abelard, (N.Y. 1970)

Greenaway, G.W., Arnold of Brescia (Cambridge 1931)

Hamilton, Bernard, Monastic Reform, Catharism and
the Crusades (London 1979)

Haskins, Charles Homer, The Renaissance of the
Twelfth Century
(Harvard 1927)

Heer, Friedrich, The Medieval World: Europe 1100-
1350 tr. J. Bonheimer (London 1962)

Holmes, U.T., Daily Living in the Twelfth Century
(Wisconsin 1956)

Hunt, Noreen, Cluny Under Saint Hugh 1049-1109
(Univ. N.Dak. 1968)

Hymnal 1940 (N.Y. 1940)

Jolivet Jean, Arts du langage et théologie chez
Abélard (Paris 1969)

Kelly, Amy, Eleanor of Aquitaine and the Four Kings
(Harvard 1950)

Knowles, David, The Evolution of Medieval Thought
(London 1962)
——————— From Pachomius to Ignatius
(Oxford 1966)

Kritzeck, James, Peter the Venerable and Islam
(Princeton 1964)

Lauchert, Friedrich, Geschichte der Physiologus (Geneva 1974)

Leclercq, Jean, St. Bernard et l'esprit cistercien (Paris 1966)

_____ Etudes sur le vocabulaire monastique (Paris 1961)

Leff, Gordon, Medieval Thought (Penguin 1958)

Lekai, Louis, The Cistercians (Kent State U. 1977)

Lindsay, T.F., St. Benedict, His Life and Work (London 1949)

Lubac, Henri de, Exégèse Médiévale (Aubier 1959) vol. 1

Luscombe, D.E., Peter Abelard's 'Ethics' (Oxford 1971)

_____ The School of Peter Abelard (Cambridge 1969)

Mabillon, J., ed., Life and Works of St. Bernard tr. J. Eales (London 1939), vol. II

Mâle, Emile, Religious Art in France in the Thirteenth Century tr. Dora Nussey (Paris 1913)

McCallum, J.R., Abelard's Christian Theology (Oxford 1948)

McLaughlin, T.P., "The Prohibition of Marriage Against Canons in the Early Twelfth Century." in Medieval Studies (Toronto 1941), vol. 3, pp. 99-100

Mohrmann, Christine, Liturgical Latin (Washington D.C. 1957)

Moore, R.I., The Origins of European Dissent (Penguin 1977)

Muckle, J.T., The Story of Abelard's Asversities (Toronto 1964)

Murray, A.V., _Abelard and St. Bernard_ (Manchester 1967)

Norbert, Dag, _Introduction à l'étude de la versifica-
tion latine médiévale_ (Stockholm 1958)

Panofsky, Erwin, _Abbot Suger and the Church of St.
Denis and its Art Treasures_
(Princeton 1946)

Peters, Edward, ed., _Heresy and Authority in Medi-
eval Europe_ (U. Penn 1980)

Pirenne, Henri, _Medieval Cities_ (Princeton 1925)

Power, Eileen, _Medieval Women_ (Cambridge 1975)

Raby, F.J.E., _Christian Latin Poetry_ (Oxford 1927)

Rashdall, H., _The Medieval Universities_ rev. Powicke
and Emden (Oxford 1936)

Riché, Pierre, _Education and Culture in the Barbarian
West_ (U. So.Car. 1976)

Rörig, Fritz, _The Medieval Town_ (Berkeley 1967)

Russell, J.B., _Dissent and Reform in the Early Mid-
dle Ages_ (U. Cal. 1965)

Schillebeeckx, Edward, _The Eucharist_ tr. D.T. Smith
(London 1968)

Silvestre, H., "A propos d'une édition récente de
l'_Hymnarius Paraclitensis_ d'Abélard,"
in _Scriptorium_ 32, 1978, pp. 91-100

Smalley, Beryl, "Stephen Langton and the Four Senses
of Scripture," in _Speculum_ 6, 1931,
pp. 60-76

_____ _The Study of the Bible in the Middle
Ages_ (Oxford 1952)

_____ ed., _Trends in Medieval Political
Thought_ (Oxford 1965) pp. 42-64

Southern, R.W., "The Letters of Abelard and Eloise,"
in Medieval Humanism and Other
Studies (N.Y. 1970)

_____ The Making of the Middle Ages.
(London 1953)

_____ Western Views of Islam in the Middle
Ages (Harvard 1962)

_____ "Dicta Anselmis," with F. S. Schmitt,
in Memorials of St. Anselm
(London 1969)

Stäblein, Bruno, Monumenta Monodica Medii Aevi
(Kassel 1956), Band 1

Storrs, Richard S., Bernard of Clairvaux (N.Y. 1912)

Stuard, S.M., Women in Medieval Society (U.Penn 1976)

Taylor, Henry Osborn, The Medieval Mind (Harvard
1962) 2 vol.

Thompson, J.W., The Literacy of the Laity in the
Middle Ages (N.Y. 1960)

Tierney, Brian, Crisis of Church and State
(N.Y. 1965)

Vacant, A., Dictionnaire de théologie catholique
(DTC) (Paris 1925-1937), vols. 1,6,13

Villehardouin & Joinville, Memoirs of the Crusades
ed. Sir Frank Marzials
(Everyman 1908)

Vogüé, Adalbert de, La Règle de Saint Benoît, tr.
Jean Neufville (Paris 1972)

Waddell, Chrysogonus, "Origin and Early Evolution
of the Cistercian Antiphon-
ary," in M. Basil Pennington,
ed., The Cistercian Spirit,
(Shannon 1970)

_____ "Peter Abelard as Creator of
Liturgical Texts,"

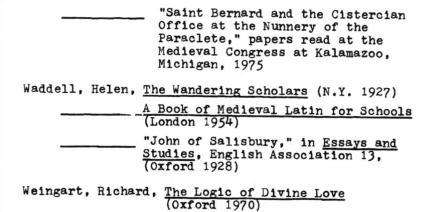

"Saint Bernard and the Cistercian Office at the Nunnery of the Paraclete," papers read at the Medieval Congress at Kalamazoo, Michigan, 1975

Waddell, Helen, The Wandering Scholars (N.Y. 1927)

_____ A Book of Medieval Latin for Schools (London 1954)

_____ "John of Salisbury," in Essays and Studies, English Association 13, (Oxford 1928)

Weingart, Richard, The Logic of Divine Love (Oxford 1970)